T0208547

# Clarity is Divine

## The Light of His Love Revealed

♥ ♥ ♥ ♥

# KELSI MARIE

WESTBOW
PRESS
A DIVISION OF THOMAS NELSON

Scripture taken from the *Amplified Bible*, Copyright © 1954, 1958, 1962, 1964, 1965, 1987 by The Lockman Foundation. Used by permission.

Scripture taken from the King James Version of the Bible.

All Scripture quotations in this publications are from **The Message**. Copyright (c) by Eugene H. Peterson 1993, 1994, 1995, 1996, 2000, 2001, 2002. Used by permission of NavPress Publishing Group.

WestBow Press books may be ordered through booksellers or by contacting:

WestBow Press
A Division of Thomas Nelson
1663 Liberty Drive
Bloomington, IN 47403
www.westbowpress.com
1 (866) 928-1240

ISBN: 978-1-4908-1268-7 (sc)
ISBN: 978-1-4908-1269-4 (hc)
ISBN: 978-1-4908-1270-0 (e)

Library of Congress Control Number: 2013918573

Printed in the United States of America.

WestBow Press rev. date: 11/12/2013

*In memory of my father, Andrew J. Arceneaux III (1947-2012) and to the glory of my Father in Heaven.*

# ACKNOWLEDGMENTS

There is nothing greater than love. I am so grateful for the love of my God. My words cannot express my appreciation for His willingness to send His guiltless son to die for the remission of my sins. I rest knowing He will never leave me.

*Mommy*, words cannot express my gratitude for your unwavering love. Thank you for believing, encouraging, supporting, motivating and cheering. My love for you exceeds the capacity of my heart.

*Ryan*, we love one another in a way that only a brother and sister can. Thank you for your support and motivation throughout this project. I love you.

*Tereva*, you're an incredible woman, an awesome mother and a little sister I have grown to admire. May the words on these pages inspire you towards your best life and give you perspective about our family history.

*Elijah*, auntie (Ta-Ta) loves you and when I tell you that you can do anything with the help of God, I'm going to refer you to this book that completely took me by surprise.

*Mo. Ann*, words cannot express my gratitude. As I tell you often, He sent you there, at that time, to save my life! I love you.

*Auntie Joann*, thank you for the history lessons, conversations and your willingness to allow me to share. If one person's life is changed, it's worth it. I love you dearly.

*Evangelist Samele A. Thorner (Mele)*, you may be the only person that can readily identify the events in this book. As I wrote, I could remember your comments, tears, anger and facial expressions when you wanted to take me and hide me, but trusted God with the process instead. Thank you for your loyalty. You have never stopped believing that good would come out of all of it.

*Min. Linda Helton* (sounds so formal). Mom, thank you. Thank you for the seeds planted. Thank you for taking the time to give scriptures to, and cultivate the faith of a young college girl. THANK YOU for walking the walk in front of my eyes, showing me the power of an effective witness!

*Evangelist Rein Johnson*, because you were willing to share, I was able to accomplish His will concerning this matter. Who would have thought years ago, that we would be *here*? I love you sis.

*First Lady Murray*, thank you for your Monday night prayers that gave me an appetite for intercession. You spoke to me so many years ago that I would walk out my purpose in strong intercession. I never forgot and God watered the seed.

*Pastor Dion Evans*, it was because you invited me to write for your blog that I began to ask the Lord what I could share that would benefit someone else. It was all GOD! Thank you!!

*Professor Andrew Tonkovich*, when my parents forced me to attend the Summer Bridge program at the University of California, Irvine, I thought they were cruel to do so. But it was there where you graded my first college paper. When I saw the B-, I was crushed. You pulled me aside and told me to never abandon my bend towards creative writing, although prose would be required of me in most of my classes, thus the reason for the B-. You told me that I had natural talent. Your comment boosted my confidence and I never forgot it (and I worked on my prose). Thank you.

# FOREWORD

Spiritual battles and emotional battles are raging all around us. Without discernment into the spiritual realm, and a sufficient amount of emotional intelligence within the community of believers, the church will never grow to her position of conquering authority and maturity. Because of the operation of evil spirits, human spirits, and the Spirit of the Lord, and a lack of discernment as to which is operating in different situations, confusion seems to abound in individuals, in churches, and in pulpits around the world. Many leaders are blowing trumpets that are giving uncertain sounds regarding the work of differing spirits because they do not understand these battles themselves.

In this book, Clarity Is Divine, Kelsi Marie Arceneaux skillfully examines and exposes the usurping and manipulating interactions that many people encounter on a daily basis. Today, as never before, Christians are opening their eyes and becoming aware of the maneuvers, manipulations, and deceptions that are occurring in our operating environment. This can only be done when we engage ourselves unrelentingly in the study and appreciation of God's word.

It has been well said that in the true sense experience is not what happens to you, rather what you do with what happens to you.

All of our experiences are processed to one degree or another . . . . but they are processed best and most effectively when the word of God is the filter through which we pass them. Then and only then is the profit and learning opportunity maximized for us and the people to whom we must minister.

When we really trust God He will take us through and then He will take us up. Many times we wonder about God's calling and God's purpose for us in ministry. As we pursue this purpose our experiences often make clear what God's intent is. By God's design what we go through becomes our transportation for who we are going to be in ministry.

When we consider how concerned the Lord is for each of us to be made whole we will diligently pray for and desire wholeness in our ministry approach. Isaiah 61: 1-3 makes it clear of how vital and important emotional and spiritual healings are to those who are called to participate in ministry: consider how Jesus describes it as he defines for us his own ministry purpose . . .

¹The Spirit of the Lord GOD is upon me; because the LORD hath anointed me to preach good tidings unto the meek; he hath sent me to bind up the brokenhearted, to proclaim liberty to the captives, and the opening of the prison to them that are bound;

²To proclaim the acceptable year of the LORD, and the day of vengeance of our God; to comfort all that mourn;

³To appoint unto them that mourn in Zion, to give unto them beauty for ashes, the oil of joy for mourning, the garment of praise for the spirit of heaviness; that they might be called trees of righteousness, the planting of the LORD, that he might be glorified.

Everyone is tested by life, but only a few folk extract strength and wisdom from their most trying experiences. We call these experiences "crucible experiences".

A crucible experience is, by definition, a transformative experience through which an individual comes to a new sense of identity.

One of the most reliable indicators and predictors of true leadership potential is an individual's ability to find meaning in negative events and to learn from even the most trying circumstances.

To put it another way the skills required to conquer adversity and to emerge stronger and more committed than ever are the same ones that make for extraordinary leaders.

Some crucible experiences illuminate hidden and suppressed areas of the soul, which many times cause you to discover new capacities and coping skills. These are often among the harshest of crucibles, involving for instance, episodes of illness, violence, betrayal, prejudice, abandonment, or rejection.

Crucible experiences are opportunities for re-identification and re-certification, for taking stock of one's life and finding meaning in circumstances many people would see as daunting and potentially incapacitating. What these experiences serve to do however is to reinvigorate, and reenergize, and recharge and give new zest for living.

Adversities come in all forms and fashions and intensities.

But they must all pass through the filter of God so they can be tempered and down-sized when necessary to *ensure* that the child of God can handle it.

Some of these adversities are mild and like fine-grained sand paper and serve only to tweak your character but other adversities are like hurricanes and your first thought is that *I'm about to be demolished.*

These transforming experiences are what is called "crucible experiences".

God wants to purify your faith and he does it in the crucible of adversity.

God does not want us operating on "inherited faith".

Inherited faith is that faith that is based on your mother or father's experience.

God does not want us operating on "textbook faith".

Textbook faith is that faith that you read about and you accept it because a reputable author tells you about it and you accept it based on his experience.

The type of faith that God wants you to have however is "proven faith", tested faith, tried faith, faith that you have exercised, and faith that you have used and put to the test.

A crucible experience is capable of re-defining our paradigms and certainly causes us to re-examine our life's reference points.

The experiences that Kelsi Marie Arceneaux has had position her to speak with authority on how much one should rely on divine wisdom and insights to help us successfully navigate our operating environments.

We will never know ourselves or the people around us the way God intends until we get a true glimpse of the righteous and holy perfection that exists in Jesus our savior. Our life's reference point will determine whether we live in the reality of God's love, grace, and righteousness or whether we live a life of delusion and deception which ends in eternal disaster.

This book offers answers and keys. Jesus Himself said, "And you shall know the truth and the truth shall make you free."

Bishop Donald R. Murray
The Good Samaritan Cathedral COGIC,
Oakland, California

# TABLE OF CONTENTS

CHAPTER ONE

# What Did You Say?

AS I DROVE *through the Caldecott Tunnel in Berkeley, CA the words were simple. They were very clear in fact. The voice on the other end of the phone said, "I don't love you anymore."*

*Have you ever experienced a moment that seemed to separate your life into "Before and After"? That was my moment. At the time, I thought my path was clear. We would marry, "do ministry", build a family, grow his business and life would be as God intended-good. He told me he was SURE I was God's choice for him and that his faith had been sealed in a vision. I went against everything screaming within me to wait a while, not to rush and grow more in understanding. I ignored how he treated his ex-girlfriend, how we even got to this place (he told me they broke up, but her version was that I "stole" him), I ignored his addiction to various women, and his proclivity towards fibbing. I ignored his mood swings and how inconsistent he was with me. He asked me to believe in him, not to give up on him and I obliged. I DECIDED that being married, settled in ministry with a clear path as a helpmeet was worth the kinks in the relationship that would be worked out in time.*

*No one advised me to examine myself to see why I would even accept such treatment and ambiguity. No one expressed to me the importance of evaluating a suitor's "character set", as you would a job applicant's skill set. No one told me that I needed to be comfortable in my own skin*

1

*or content as a single person before I even CONSIDERED marriage. Hmmmm, well, honestly, maybe if I had shared the ugly truths of the relationship, someone would have told me these things. Sometimes we don't share so that we won't have to hear the bitter truth. We'd rather remain deluded. Until that point, living single had been reduced to a season of waiting to be married. Period. This was an ideal situation, right? It was biblical, wasn't it? I was saved and so was he. I had given my life to ministry and he had too. He knew the importance of prayer and washing his wife with the word and I knew the importance of serving as a helpmeet. I was told that I needed a "covering" [needed to be married] as I embarked on ministry. Three different people had prophesied to me that this was my husband—two of them while he was still with the other young lady. I wasn't mature enough to know that such prophecies were out of order as they made me feel entitled to him, although a sister in Christ was hurting. So, when the opportunity presented itself, I threw caution to the wind. This was my LIFE. God had FINALLY revealed His plan for MY LIFE. So, I drove the car in a trance while holding the phone to my ear.*

*All I could muster was, "What did you just say? What do you mean you don't love me anymore?" All I was thinking was, "He doesn't get to say this to me." My thinking was, we're MARRIED, well, not really, but as good as married in my imagination and heart. I had committed to this! Later when he handed me a shoebox of my belongings in his driveway, I didn't cry or yell. I softly reminded him that this was HIS idea and that he had asked me to believe in him. I reminded him that I went against the warnings of my parents, my friends and the entire church was gossiping about me because of the scorned ex-girlfriend's spin on their break-up and that now he was abandoning me. He told me he had made a mistake—that he must have misinterpreted "the vision". He expressed that he wanted to go back to his ex and that after dating HER for a few more years and restoring her trust, he would marry HER and that he wished me the best. This is where I probably wanted to pinch myself. This couldn't be real, right? What is happening to MY LIFE???*

*The path that I had seen so vividly for the past few months was growing dimmer and dimmer and the door to my depression was the realization that without him, I didn't have a plan. I couldn't even remember who I was apart from the identity I had embraced as his future wife. "What am I going to do now?" . . . That is all I heard in my mind for a very long time. "What am I going to do now?" The seed of rejection had been planted and my self-esteem [already low], took a nosedive.*

*Today, I flash back to that scene and I THANK GOD!!! I am now thankful for the opportunity to acquire wisdom before becoming anyone's wife. I am grateful for the opportunity to learn my own value; and establish that God has a plan for ME, alone and independent of my role in someone else's life (Jeremiah 29:11). I embrace wholeheartedly the fact that what I perceived as rejection was actually an "ejection" from a situation that was not God's best for me. I cannot imagine who I would have become if I had operated in a marriage as deficient as I was in godly wisdom and understanding.*

*I will share with you several of the things I have learned:*

- You never want to build a relationship on someone else's back. No matter what story he or she tells you, if another person is still hurt, you probably need to probe a little deeper into the situation to see where there are loose ends and if something was handled inappropriately. If he/she betrayed the last person, they will likely do the same to you. Never take part in doing anything to someone else, that you wouldn't want done to you.
- Pay attention to how someone speaks of having hurt someone. Are they indifferent or callous?
- Be cautious of an individual that vacillates often, because God is NOT the author of confusion.
- Share with an accountability partner or a mentor EVERY facet of the relationship, not just the parts you aren't

embarrassed to tell. Emotions can impede your ability to make sound decisions.

- Pray fervently and consistently for direction. We have a God who loves us to the point that He will steer us around potholes and reveal things that are hidden to the natural eye. If a person is not right for you, He WILL reveal it. It is your job to heed the warning.

- Yield your desire to be married to Him, being resolved that you will hold out for His best for you. We must remember that He knows not only where we are, but where we are going and He will give us a mate that can accommodate both.

- Timing is EVERYTHING. To be out of God's timing is to be out of His will. When He says "not yet", that is exactly what He means.

- Never invest in a relationship on a spousal level until you are a spouse.

- Finally, be committed to bringing out the best in someone and aiding them in being the best servant or maidservant they can be for Christ; keeping that in mind will help you to resist sexual temptation. When you make a decision to be on the Lord's side, you don't want to be the person luring them into sin.

*Sometimes I sit back and wonder what I ever did to deserve being spared a very painful marriage and then I realize it wasn't anything I earned. Hey, I was ALL in, remember? I cried [some] long nights for many years. I felt cursed, forgotten and unlovable. The seed of rejection flourished into a plant that made my progress stagnate; however, growing in Christ has changed my perspective. For every embarrassing time I had to express to someone that "it didn't work out", I am now very thankful. I desire that my marriage be built on a strong, solid foundation in the word of God. And I wish the same for you. The word of God tells me what He wants for me in a husband (1Peter 3, Ephesians 5). And now*

*I am confident [in Him] that I will recognize it when I see it. God is CERTAINLY good and* **Clarity is Divine**.

That's it—this article was the inspiration for this book. After writing it I couldn't understand why it got the attention it did. Why was it such a big deal? People responded to me as if I had walked through fire or something. But, I guess I did. It's interesting to me because it was nothing new to me; it was my story. It was one of the episodes in my relationship with *him*. The true purpose of the article was not to draw attention to the Caldecott Experience, but to get the word out there to other women about what I **learned** from the relationship. There is so much hurt we endure that could be avoided.

I shared nine points in the article that can help any of us avoid building a relationship void of integrity. Having a Godly relationship is like being pregnant. Either it is Godly or it isn't. There is no middle ground. You aren't almost pregnant or pregnant most of the time with a slip here and there. And at the end of a courtship—whether the courtship ends in marriage or by dissolution, it was either Godly or it wasn't. It was done His way or by way of the flesh, but not both. There is no such thing as mostly pure or 99% pure. It's 100% pure or not pure at all.

If you are in a relationship with someone and in your bliss, you are aware there is someone devastated on the other end, it should matter to you. As someone who has felt pain and cried tears, it should affect you that someone is experiencing such discomfort. I am not saying it is up to you to fix the problem or automatically avoid the opportunity for the new relationship. What I am saying is investigate—ask questions-pray. I am always weary of someone who, in their recollection of the demise of their past relationship, takes NO responsibility. That just isn't realistic. Even if someone's error was making a bad decision based on lust, emotion, desperation, dysfunction or insecurity, they should own it! It is never ALL one person's fault. Even if the fault someone has to accept is making poor decisions. It is important to pay attention to how our suitor responds to the fact that someone is in pain. If they are indifferent simply because their interest has waned, you can expect that given the same outcome, you won't get much consideration either. It's indicative of a character flaw. Who wants to establish a future with a person that is incapable of feeling sympathy? I am not at all saying that their sympathy should motivate them to stay connected to an individual, but hopefully they are at least truly apologetic (and have communicated it to the individual) for being responsible in any way for their discomfort. It is possible to be sympathetic without accepting blame. As women one of the worst mistakes me make is being callous when it comes to the feelings of another woman—a SISTER in Christ. No matter what her "issues", she is a sister. Besides, you have your own set of issues as well. I shall never forget an adage my grandmother used to quote, "Never look down on a woman scorned, but comfort her in her sorrow, 'cause it's a cold, cold, cold world and you could be down tomorrow."

I warned against being emotionally connected to an individual that vacillates often. James 1:3 states that "A double-minded man is unstable in all of his ways." Someone who has trouble making decisions has trouble making decisions. I don't know how to put that any simpler. The person that is always all over the place and whose emotions have the stability of water will be the same person that will be in love with you one day and over you the next. Not being able to predict whether you have a place in their world from one day to the next is not only emotionally exhausting, it chips away at your ability to depend on them and feel any level of security in the relationship. And when we don't feel secure, we don't feel safe. Why settle for a situation where you don't feel safe?

Accountability partners aide us in keeping perspective and our emotions in check. When prayerfully considering marriage and our emotions are leading, God isn't. Despite indicators, warning lights, sirens, bells and whistles, we will continue to move full speed ahead as a response to the warmth of companionship. Too often we avoid sharing details that a level-headed person might consider a warning.

It's our way of avoiding what we know. If we honestly feel nothing is wrong, we wouldn't hide it. If we go into the courtship determined to maintain integrity, we will keep it in the direct light of God's word instead of allowing *secrets* to lurk in the shadows. Again, the purpose of the accountability partner isn't to be judgmental or unforgiving, but to help us keep proper perspective. And someone who isn't emotionally invested in the relationship can be helpful in doing so. The relationship in which you're investing doesn't have to be perfect, but it does need to be clean and honest.

Many people are ideal for the season, the summer or the school year. But in time, it can become evident that their intentions aren't our intentions or their life plan doesn't accommodate ours or vice-versa. Some opportunities present themselves in a split second—opportunities that can create a fork in the road where one person is led to go left and the other person to go right. Since only God knows where He will lead us and exactly what our future consists of, doesn't it seem necessary to allow Him to direct us in marital decisions? There are bad options, good options, and then there are His best options for us. What happens if a choice someone makes down the line completely derails the life of someone committed to Christ? Only God knows this will happen at the onset of your interest in the person. And His present "no" can keep your divine future a "yes". We have to trust Him to be the Father that steers us around potholes and helps us to avoid terrain that can permanently disable us.

In Godliness, there is order. Our standard is His word and His righteousness. We hear so often about the will of God being our safest place. It is essential we do our part. His timing isn't always convenient, but it is certainly perfect. Too soon, too late, too fast, or too slow will move us out of His timing and eventually out of His will. We have to remain sensitive to Him and obey His directives for the various seasons of our lives.

A wife is a wife and a husband is a husband. There are concessions and sacrifices associated with each role, and there is safety in the mutual sacrifices made *as unto the Lord*. We obey scripture with regard to our mates, and God honors and blesses the roles He has ordained that honor and bless Him. We cannot expect Him to guard from the enemy, what *we* contaminate with the works of the enemy. When we include the enemy, we choose the enemy. You either commit the relationship to God and rely on his sovereignty, or you compromise, step out of order, thus out of His will; and then ask Him to fix what you left Him out of at your convenience. The problem is, no matter how well you think things will turn out, when you play on the enemy's playground, he cheats, he lies and he doesn't give the ball back when he says he will. He not only aims to make sure you lose the game, he aims to injure you so you can't play at all.

Throughout our "pre-Christ" relationships, we've cheated. We have invited the enemy in by being to boyfriends and girlfriends what God only intended for us to be to someone in the context of marriage. We have made sacrifices with a false selflessness that doesn't glorify God, but caters to the flesh; the results of which have been detrimental. We have suffered heartaches, lost identities, self-confidence and sacrificed emotional stability. We can never forget we have an adversary. He has used the things and people we thought we wanted, to lure us away from God's order, and the resulting emotional trauma has slowly chipped away at our souls. Without a transformed mind, we cannot fathom HOW enduring the discomfort of doing it differently (His way) can turn out well. Thus, we stay in abusive cycles.

Why on Earth would there be a boyfriend that betrays you five or ten times? The first time should be enough. And if you follow the lessons that I learned—that I wrote about, then you certainly won't have to ENDURE such excruciating circumstances. But I had to get CLEAR. I didn't "get it" for quite some time. The relationship wasn't truly over the day of the Caldecott experience, nor were the lessons understood the next week. No, it took time and a LOT more heartbreak. I wasn't done, hardly; no way. I would endure this madness for YEARS to come.

# CHAPTER TWO

## *Part Deux*

DON'T BE ANGRY about what happened to me in the Caldecott Tunnel. Be angry that I wasn't DONE. Be angry when he came back I took him. Be angry I can't honestly tell you how many more times in the course of the relationship I endured the "Caldecott Experience". Be angry about the fact that YEARS later on the day of his wedding, when I had FINALLY stopped taking his calls and he had FINALLY stuck with a choice, I cried in a fetal position the ENTIRE day. Be angry I STILL felt like I had lost. Hopefully, you'll be angry enough to assassinate the mindset that influences us to accept anything less than God's best for our lives. Kill the mindset on sight. Kill it in yourself, in your loved ones, in him, in her and wherever else it appears. We MUST speak up when we see others headed down the same path that almost destroyed us.

Why do we do it? In any other context, would the definition be masochism? We say it hurts, but we stay. Why do we do that? We cry, threaten to leave, tremble, yell, "check 'em", but then stay. WHY do we do it? It comes in different forms and circumstances, but it's all the same. Mine may play out with me telling him I know my value; I deserve better; I've been too good to him to be treated this way and that I will NOT stand for it. Yours may have played out with you begging them not to leave you, asking them to [just] tell you what you have to do and you will fix it.

One of you may have found out about ANOTHER betrayal at the doctor's office where you heard yourself say, "I have a what?!" And you were too embarrassed to admit that the only person you had been sleeping with was your . . . And maybe your recollection of the incident fades with the memory of leaving the doctor's office in shame, getting to your car and weeping loudly from the blow that has you feeling like you will NEVER recover.

Oh, but there's another sister who is badly bruised inside and out. Her eyes are bloodshot from being choked; her ribs hurt, her arms are bruised, her head is pounding and through her rapid breathing and trembling body, she SWEARS she'll never go back to him.

What about the brother who just punched a hole in the wall because he has NEVER been what she's accused him of being? He's paid her rent, accepted her abuse, and stumbled upon pictures in her cell phone that were NOT sent to him. He's the OPPOSITE of the man most women complain about. He's the one who went to work, helped her out in every way possible, remembered birthdays and really was the best man he could be; and he is now saying to himself: "She stepped out again?" Or better yet, "This one cheated too?"

There's also you, the sister who receives a call from your girlfriend telling you that she saw "him" at the "swanky" place with "her" [the other her], eating a "surf & turf" and through your tears and headache, all you can think about is EVERYTHING you've doled out. You've cooked, you've cleaned, you've encouraged, you've sexed, birthed, aborted and yet YOU weren't worth a steak and lobster?! Why is a stranger who has nothing invested "worth" more than you?

The scenarios change like the weather. We ALL have a story. Let's take the focus off of the offender and answer the aforementioned question: Why do we do that? After making empty threats that I wouldn't tolerate being mistreated and would leave him, why did I pick up the phone and **call**? After leaving the doctor, why did you confront him in anger DEMANDING to know xyz when all that should have mattered was you had contracted a sexually transmitted disease? Why did you beg someone to stay who made it clear they wanted to leave? Why did you walk past the mirror, look at your battered and bruised reflection and OPEN THE DOOR for the one who had your blood on his hands? Why were you paying her rent knowing you were checking her phone every chance you got? And finally, WHY did you feel the need to REMIND him of everything you've done for him when you KNOW he hadn't forgotten?

Why do we do it? Whyyyyy do we do it? Why do we sell ourselves short? Why do we give our ALL in response to getting very little? Why do we fear the pain of being without more than we hate being mistreated? It's a serious question because being mistreated really does hurt. So again, why do we do it?

Don't be deceived. If you have experienced ANY of the pain I've described as a result of accepting less than what you've deserved, it is imperative that you find the answer to THE question. If you don't DEAL [with it], you won't HEAL [from it]. It isn't fair when the person who damaged you the most was loved by a better version of you; and the person who is better for you is forced to work with the jaded leftovers of the person you used to be. Shouldn't you be your best for the person who is best for you?

What if the mate you have dreamed of is in the wings somewhere waiting for you to love yourself? What if God's blessing is being withheld until you lose your appetite for toxicity? What if God is simply waiting for you to love Him enough to keep His commandments?

Driving home one night, after another verbal assault to my esteem, I cried out to the Lord. I whimpered and whined about how badly I was being treated. I was arrested by an epiphany that I still believe I heard. I don't want to smear the focus of this story by getting into a theological debate about whether or not the Holy Spirit quoted a line out of Star Trek. But this revelation that I heard stopped me "mid-whimper": "There is no honor amongst thieves."

My entire perspective changed at that moment. I understood that I had violated God's principles and was in turn crying to Him that I had been violated. It was as absurd as the thought of you stealing from a person only to run home and find the same person was at your house stealing from you; and you complaining to the police with the object you stole still in your hand.

I had to take responsibility for my actions and shift my allegiance to the word and will of God. We leave ourselves open to all kinds of assaults when through deliberate sin in our lives we have stepped out from under the covering of obedience. Many of us have to look at our past or present situations and admit fault. We must take responsibility for granting access to the enemy of our souls through actions that oppose God's word. And trust that once the enemy makes it in, he wants to wreak havoc.

Honoring Godly principles keeps us blessed, righteous (in right standing with Him), and safe. When our aim is pleasing Him and obeying Him out of love instead of what we will get out of it, our appetites begin to change. One may argue their interpretation of Psalm 37:4 as, we get what we want (our desires) when we delight ourselves in Him, but my conviction is that when we delight ourselves in Him, thus losing ourselves in Him, our desires for ourselves line up with His desires for us and we are granted them. In other words, just lose yourself in seeking God and you will end up in a much more fulfilling place.

Whether you're currently in "a situation" or have been delivered out of one, my prayer for us is that we will do the work required to be the BEST that we can be. Build upon your prayer life. Increase your time in the word of God. Ask Him to reveal to you the personal tendencies that landed you in relationships that didn't reflect self-love or God's love for you. Allow the spirit of God to BANISH the fear that seduced you into thinking you couldn't have better. All of us have "a story", but we triumph when we embrace the lessons we've learned and eventually end up in better shape than before we entered the relationship. If you're reading this, you have survived. This is your opportunity to be stronger and wiser. What was meant to subtract from you actually positioned you for wonderful additions to your life! I encourage you to strip pain of its power by dancing in your victory and singing in your success. We are more than conquerors through Him who loved us (Romans 8:37)! God is CERTAINLY good. Accountability is honest. And **Clarity is Divine.**

Remember how I kept asking "Why Do We Do it"? Before I could trust myself in a relationship—even trust myself to identify the mate for the marriage I know God wants for me, I had to find the answer to that question. Why did he matter so much? Why did I try so hard? Why did I want the relationship so badly?

The short answer to the question would obviously be that I didn't think enough of myself. But what was the long answer? What was the genesis of this absence of self-worth? After going back through some old journals that at one point I wanted to burn, I was able to get a better snapshot of what my thought patterns were when I was in bondage. I'll share one...brace yourself:

*January 17, 2006*

*To Whomever Cares,*

*I don't want to go through life in drudgery. It seems as though there are certain constants which have remained. And I study these constants—I study my involvement and then I have to accept the fact that I'm partially responsible. There was a time in college when I was so miserable, I was so alone. When it came time for everyone to go home after whatever activity—they would go to a home, to a husband. Some would go home to a boyfriend—just someone who cared. And I remember living in dread then. I remember wanting to be embraced, loved, cared for, supported, wanted. I hated my life then. I remember asking God to lead me to a church where I could be active. I wanted to be involved. Most of all, I think I wanted to be understood. My family didn't understand me. My family (immediate) loves me, but to this day, I can't say they understand.*

*Now, some nine years since college, I'm not better. Actually, I'm worse. I probably have less dignity now, less self-respect. I hate myself because of what I've contributed to my life. There's something about me, something within me, that sabotages any chances of being fully embraced and understood. The inner conflict is that while it is a deep, sincere, nearly breathtaking yearning, something in my other half will not allow it to be cultivated. There's a part of me somewhere, in some faculty that causes people to be repulsed. How else can I want something so badly and those who push it away and/or abuse it, are the ones who receive it-all because there's too much to go around. I've failed. I've failed. I've failed at life, I've failed at love and I've failed at having the ability to be loved. When I kept myself, I wasn't loved. When I shared myself, I wasn't loved. I'm not even considered. My heart isn't considered. My presence isn't considered, my feelings aren't considered. They show me over and over that I'm not worth the investment. You know, it's worse now because it's easy to look forward to receiving the love you need in the household of faith. Perhaps it's the let down that hurts more than the void. And what gives the let down such gravity, such pull, such force is the hope that it destroyed. Just DESTROYED my hope. I reflect and think—I thought this could happen for me. I thought, I really thought I could be loved. I really thought there was a better life for me. So, if it isn't in the church, if it isn't among seasoned saints who know what love is and how to love, then perhaps my safe place doesn't even exist.*

*I'm alone. And I wasn't created to be. Yet of all the seeds that have been sown, this is the one that life has nurtured. I feel like if I don't die, I'll lose my mind. Aren't there those who receive such an outpouring of love, that it completely breaks them and humbles them because they can't imagine what they've done to receive it? I'm not perfect—nowhere near it, but because I want it so badly, because it isn't a bad thing that I want, can I not have it? Why, why is the answer no? Why does this happen for me like this? At least can I know why it has to hurt so badly? Why do I have to miss it? There is absolutely no concern-none at all. Does God care or realize that if my life isn't going to be any better than this, it will break my heart that He makes me stay, that He requires me to live? That would make me feel like He doesn't love me at all. I guess I need to be completely re-wired. A new mind, a new heart, a new past, a new present, new options, new opportunities. I think I'm dead already where it really matters. And having to walk this out is just salt to the wounds. I hate this. I just hate it so much. Somebody who is right in the mind, soul and spirit could have a wonderful life with my able body and other great physical things God has bestowed on me. There are people who don't have the activity of their limbs. There are people who are happy, have a great personality and do so much with life, yet wish they looked just a little better. Everything I am, hides between church and home. What a waste. I don't know how to function anywhere else. I'm not comfortable being who I am. Eventually the façade would have to come down and everyone would know that I'm this messed up.*

I remember that place. It was a bad place, a dark place, a low place. I felt like I was living my life grieving, but no one had died. It seemed as if my recurring thoughts were, "God is good, yet I'm not. I'm really messed up. I don't know how to be better. When is it all going to be over with?"

There was this longing I had—a longing to be loved by someone who wasn't obligated to love me. I mean an emotional love. A love you CHOOSE to have for someone. I felt that would be proof that I was lovable. I look back now and realize just how much God's love wasn't enough for me. Now I understand that it was because my mind hadn't been transformed—I hadn't elevated His truth about me over my opinion and circumstances. He wasn't the Lord of my MIND. I took for granted that God loved me, because He loves everybody. It didn't seem personal. I think I just wanted to be "worthy of selection". I didn't see the value in the fact that He chose ME! I knew my parents and my brother loved me, but they were my parents and brother.

Now I look back at how I even took that for granted. What I was searching for at that time was asinine, or did it even exist. The sense of belonging that I wanted to feel—the validation that I craved could really only come from one source. Yet, I discarded it. Oh my religious self would have said that it wasn't so—but it was.

Take inventory of just how often we seek approval from man before God. After you preach—after you sing—after you share a thought or perspective. If you felt God was the only one who was pleased, it would seem like an epic failure. We WANT to be validated and crave the pats on the back. It just doesn't seem to count if someone doesn't endorse it.

I thought having the love and acceptance from people would be enough, but it would not have been sufficient. Because even if I had the affection and acceptance from the people I wanted it from, it would have been a fractured and damaging love—a philos love; not one that restores, covers and brings a person to wholeness. Insecure, emotionally damaged people cannot love perfectly. The love they give is marred by their fragmented disposition. A person covered in mud from head to toe, including their extremities cannot hand you a white t-shirt without staining it. Whatever they touch (in this case, fingertips to grains of fabric) is marred by what covers them. If someone is controlling, I'm only going to feel their love as long as I allow them to control me. They won't validate me any other time. If a person is insecure, I'm their best companion, while I'm stroking their ego and accommodating their need for validation. And if a person is damaged emotionally, they will guard themselves against anything I may be that is remotely reminiscent of their painful past. That is a fractured love—a broken love. So, how can it restore or make whole a person who is fractured and broken themselves?

# CHAPTER THREE

# *Broken Thoughts*

MY WORLD WAS small and my pain was deep.

Since the limits of my immediate surroundings were indicative to me of the limits of the world at large, I put all of my proverbial eggs into one proverbial basket. All I knew was family—extended family and in my estimation, I had failed to be lovable there. So now appears a new alternative for acceptance—God; only that meant to me—*church*. I didn't realize that they were two very different things. I am not referring to His body in its entirety or His kingdom, but rather protocols and personalities of a local assembly. It never dawned on me that rejections in the building wouldn't guarantee rejection elsewhere. I had to be validated THERE (my local assembly)—I had to be accepted THERE because that place was the demonstration of God—all I knew about God. If I didn't make it there, if I failed there, I failed with God. And if I didn't even have acceptance in Christ (notice I didn't say BY Christ), I might as well go buy myself a casket, jump in and wait to stop breathing. How I wish someone had told me to take my backpack off; that all of the hurts I packed and carried with me from childhood would stay right with me until I put them down. I wish someone had told me that because my cousins called me fat and I was never as pretty and slim as "her", I would carry with me the need to compete and prove I, too, had a space in the world and was deserving of some semblance of affection. Only, how would I prove what I didn't believe myself?

There was a seed of rejection that had been sown and watered early in my life. Now I was dealing with a prickly thorn bush that had sprouted up on the inside of me. It's a concept that I now know to be *false core beliefs*. That young lady didn't believe she was made in Christ's image. As much as she wanted companionship, she wasn't convinced she was worthy of it. Life had taught her otherwise.

I thought that the doorway to purpose had to be EARNED. Yeah, it sounds ridiculous NOW, but anyone in a pattern of self-abuse and the rut of dysfunctional relationships, understands what I am talking about. It is the same mindset that makes you sit and beg God to let your life be good—worth living—might I dare even say ENJOYABLE. And I did a lot of begging.

I looked at everyone else and thought there was some secret "middle passage" they crossed; there was just a way they were not and I was, that made it possible for them to be "loved" and me to remain "ALONE". It was almost as if there was a monkey on my back that everyone else evaded somehow. Something was keeping me out of the "goodness", so I thought. As a result, I tried harder and harder to be better. If I could just do better, I'll be better; and if I can just be better, I won't be this person. I wanted to be able to have the life Christ died for me to have. But where did all of this flawed thinking start? That is what I needed to understand. Where did I pick up the notions that I wasn't enjoyable ENOUGH; I wasn't pretty ENOUGH; I was too fat, too loud, too serious, too spiritual. I sort of wanted to undo myself; just start all over again. I found another journal entry:

*November 17, 2005*

*Father, This is the day that you have made and I shall rejoice. I shall rejoice, HALLELUJAH!!!!*

*I'm trying to make sure that I remain steadfast and do everything that I said I would do. I'm trying to make sure that I stay faithful, that*

*I treat people well. I want to be consistent. I'm just figuring that if I can get this right, if I can just get this together and please you, then you will reward me with my purpose. I want you to be pleased with me so that I can do what it is that you've put me here to do. It's important to me that as I head home, you will feel that I'm worthy of you looking at me and saying well done and that I've been good and faithful.*

*I just keep waiting for something to happen. Something, anything, to make all of this make sense. To make me feel like life is worth the pain, discouragement and disappointment that I've felt. Aren't I supposed to feel that overall, life is worth it? Why do I continue to feel that my purpose, my potential, my life, has been stolen from me? Why do I continue to feel that my enemies and the dark forces that will to keep me away from the center of your will, my purpose, my strength, have won?—That they laugh and point as I toil to find my way—Feeling void, feeling empty, feeling alone, feeling undeserving.*

*Everyday is a wait . . . . A hope that something will happen, something will occur, something will change, something will make sense. And at the end of everyday and the winding down of every night, I say to myself, tomorrow is a new day and it will be time for me to yet wait again. Maybe the Lord will show Himself strong in my life tomorrow. Maybe, my brother will be healed tomorrow, maybe my family will be in order tomorrow, maybe my father's heart will be turned towards the Lord tomorrow, maybe I'll no longer love who doesn't love me tomorrow, oh, maybe tomorrow, even he will become sensitive to what I've endured. Maybe tomorrow . . . .*

*The sin in my life is that my joy is in the hope of better times. The sin in my life is that I don't embrace today and feel that it is worth living. If I've failed at everything and conquered nothing, succeeded at nothing, mastered nothing, attained no means to care for myself, then why must I stay? I can't leave until I've completed my assignment. So every night, as I drift to sleep, I wonder, will my assignment come tomorrow? I'm embarrassed of myself. I'm embarrassed of who I am, and who I am not. Is that the real reason I don't open up, why I don't talk to anyone about what's going on? I mean, if they catch wind of what's really going on with me, they'll know that my life doesn't matter, that I have turned out a waste. A waste of investment, time, love and attention. God forbid everyone knows that about me. They'd be angry that I'm even alive— that they ever even thought I mattered. EVER.*

After reading the words in that journal entry, it is obvious that I suffered from depression. I was certainly and certifiably depressed. I spoke to no one about the deep desire to be someone different. In ministry I was productive. People came to me for answers and told me they admired my worship, were encouraged by my delivery, but as clearly as you read the words on this page, it should also be evident that I hadn't even begun to understand the concept of God's grace. It was insane for me to serve a God who I honestly felt I had to beg for an enjoyable life. Well, now that I put it *that* way, it sounds silly. But, how many of us secretly feel the reason we are suffering, the reason we are hurting, the reason we lost the job, the marriage, the friendship—the actual reason we were betrayed by our hope is because there is something wrong with us? Even when we point the finger at others, we privately point to a place within us that we have convinced ourselves is the reason it all happened.

We stay in the relationship—marriage-friendship-situation, because at the end of the day, if we're really honest, we don't blame them for treating us as badly as they do. On some level, we honestly feel we deserve it. And we sit back and imagine a God in Heaven who stands sternly with his arms crossed and watches us be penalized for an innate flaw that we seem to have no control over. Because we're Christians, we continue to hope and believe. It is what we are told to do. And because things never change, we become more and more convinced THESE things just aren't attainable to us. It isn't for a person like me—a person this peculiar, odd and abnormal or messed up. So, we exist and wait to die. Where is the victory in that? Where is the grace?

The truth is that faith cometh by hearing (Romans 10:17).

And if there is any part of you that is engaged when a sermon is being delivered, no matter how downtrodden you are, there's always a flicker of hope. There's a part of you STILL alive that says "just maybe", maybe it can happen for me too. And the tango with deception continues. Why do I call it that? Well, because you cannot earnestly hope for what you do not believe. And although the Word ignites hope, your entire existence is rooted in a false belief that you do not deserve and will not attain what is readily available to others. You leave the emotional charge of the service and resort to hopelessness at the first sign of opposition. And the vertical fall seems to hurt more and more each time. It is up to us to eventually decide God is in fact larger than our circumstances and that he has the autonomy to change them. We MUST believe!

If I really believe I am lovable, why do I tolerate such treatment? But if I really am lovable, why am I never treated any better, ever, by anyone?

If we are going to have an authentic relationship with Christ, we MUST understand a transformed mind isn't an option or a perk, but mandatory. Our core belief system has to be completely revamped. Our core beliefs serve as the foundation of our operating system. It starts in childhood and the concrete is poured slowly and steadily, and is reinforced over time. There are pillars that hold up the framework of our minds. We aren't even capable of being our authentic selves with the old framework because that framework was shaped in iniquity and born in sin (Psalms 51:5). There had never been any consultation with the Creator with regard to who we are or what we were created to be; that framework was built simply as a response to the jarring emotional stimuli and abuses of life. Upon becoming a new creature, this foundation contends with the word of God to sit on the throne of our hearts. We conveniently lay scriptures on top of our old wicked foundation. We smear the sermons we've heard on top of it, and we try to build a new life with Christ on a foundation our adversary laid. No wonder I was so messed up.

The concrete of a foundation has to be violently broken. Even concrete that was poured with objects that obstruct its integrity hardens. The *Caldecott Experience* wasn't the jackhammer that began to break up the foundation. It was merely the charge given to the jackhammer. I would have to go back—way back to figure out when and why I became the person that would settle for this relationship, this treatment and the belief system that communicated it was the best I could have. Each memory would need to be exposed to the jackhammer and completely cracked apart and overwritten. What God says about me, his plans for me and my future would have to replace the perspective that I initially internalized as a result of my experiences.

# CHAPTER FOUR

## Set in Stone

OUR CORE BELIEF system is etched in the walls of our mind and heart. It's what we build from and the system we use to process life. It's our paradigm, our filter. Think about it.

I'll compare three different young women with different core belief systems. *Casey* grew up in a Christian home. Her parents were very loving towards one another and they raised her in the fear of the Lord. Her parents had a system and structure in their marriage where certain duties were the responsibility of her mother and others, her father. They committed to the structure and honored it. They were kind to one another. When we were in college, Casey shared that she was still a virgin and she had never departed from what her parents had taught her. She wanted a marriage like her parents'. And as she had various suitors, she wasn't desperate; she was extremely cautious, in fact. She wasn't a casual dater and she knew that casual dating wouldn't yield the results she wanted. Her ultimate goal wasn't to be someone's "girlfriend", nor was it to avoid being alone. She was disciplined, studied hard and had a belief that if she did what she was supposed to do, she could trust God to uphold His end of the bargain. I wasn't saved at the time and I remember staring at her as she prayed EVERY morning and EVERY night. Guess what? Casey avoided a lot of heartache that many of us young ladies experienced throughout our college years. She had core beliefs that were grounded in the word of God and she would not compromise; these beliefs ended up protecting her. In the end, there was a reward.

There was another friend from college, who I will call *Tammy*. She was kind, attractive and was the young lady we all knew to go from long-term relationship to long-term relationship. She, too, came from a home with a healthy marriage. Her parents' marriage had a strong sense of companionship and loyalty as far as she knew. As she wanted to emulate her parents, she felt her place was in a RELATIONSHIP. She also chose not to be a casual dater. Although she fornicated, she limited it to the confines of a "relationship". For the record, I am not at all presenting this as a biblical model.

Tammy met a young man very soon after coming to the university and was with the same person for quite some time. At some point she found out that he had cheated on her in the past. Immediately she broke up with him. Two weeks later, after crying and toiling, she emerged from her dorm room, ten pounds lighter (from not eating) and resolved that he wasn't worth her affection. She never allowed him back into her personal space. There was a core belief she had that she was deserving of loyalty and anyone who couldn't extend it to her wasn't worth her companionship.

The next young lady I would like you to consider is *Kendra*. She was conceived in an extra-marital affair. Although her father provided financial support, he wasn't engaged emotionally. His wife and kids didn't know about Kendra and she was aware she was a "secret". She knew about her sisters and brothers and often bragged on the playground about her half siblings. She was well aware she didn't receive nearly the same amount of focus and attention her half siblings received from her father. And often times she had to deal with the anguish of longing for a family that didn't even know she existed. As a young adult, Kendra stayed in a relationship with her daughter's father knowing far too often she was the "other" woman. There were multiple promises of marriage, but no follow through. She is STILL in a relationship with someone who doesn't value her enough and has eaten ten years of her young adult life.

Her circumstances growing up never communicated to her she deserved better or she was worth more. Just as Kendra starved for her father's affection, she continues to starve for the affection of the man in her life.

I provided these real life scenarios to demonstrate just how much our core beliefs play out in our lives. And unless overwritten, we act out as adults, the core beliefs that we embraced during our childhood. Each of the young women I mentioned is attractive and intelligent. They are wonderful mothers and immensely talented. They are each very loving and have a wealth of attributes to offer to any marriage, yet because of their core beliefs, their outcomes are quite different. Not one of the young women is better than the other, but a couple of the women think better of themselves. There are circumstances and conditions that they aren't willing to accept, based on their levels of self worth.

What will our lives look like when we become resolved and refuse to accept any less than what God has willed for us? Imagine what life will look like when there are conditions we refuse to accept based on what our Father has whispered to us about whom we are and what He has predestined for us? The "whisper" is found in the Word of God. The whisper is what He says about you. It is what He says you can have. It reinforces your worth based on the sacrifice (His son) made for you. And any time you see yourself as less than what He says you are, your core beliefs are in complete opposition to His Word.

Whatever has been ministered to your core—good or bad—whether in thought, word or deed, tends to not only become a core belief, but manifests itself socially. Many women who endure being treated poorly haven't merely accepted it, nor half-heartedly embraced it; but often times they are in a relationship they have fought to hold on to. There's a fear of "losing" which stems from the fact they don't believe they can ever attract better. They don't know anything else, so what other expectation can they fathom, except by faith?

These are the women who, as I have, live in a prison of fear, insecurity and comparison. There are women who will endure emotional and/or physical abuse for fear that if they don't, they won't be able to replace the betrayer of her trust. She doesn't know or expect another, a better source of security. In her core belief system is the absence of the revelation of God's love.

In my search for clarity, for accountability sake, I had to draw understanding from various relational scenarios. I had to accept the fact that everything didn't happen TO me. There are some situations we walk into *eyes wide open*. I had to ask what it was about Casey that granted her a more peaceful and fulfilling young adult experience. Her core beliefs shaped a behavioral model for her and from her first relationship on through marriage, she carried herself with a certain confidence. She may not be the woman that is constantly looking over her shoulder and checking her husband's cell phone. She's being the wife she's learned to be from her mother and she's expecting nothing less than what she saw her father model at home. She had a father who looked forward to seeing her, listened to how her day went and told her that she was beautiful. And as a result, she grew up confident she would be the bright spot of someone's day, convinced that what she has to say is important and she deserves someone who is appreciative of her physical appearance and presence. As a result, she made decisions from this platform of her self image.

These are three women with three different belief systems, which created completely different realities. There are those who feel they deserve the best and those who feel they don't. It is not about believing that you are better than anyone else; it's just about believing you deserve better. In order to uproot and begin breaking up the core beliefs that have misled us, we must conduct an introspective search and get clear about how we really feel about ourselves and what fears are motivating us. The truth is that *perfect love casts out fear.* (1 John 4:18) If we had a true revelation of God's perfect love we would place His love on top of every thought, insecurity and fear. Every fear of being rejected, alone, not good enough, not pretty enough, not successful enough, not loved enough would be cast out, never to return. But at our core, we've believed something very different about ourselves.

This brings me to a list of core beliefs that antagonize a healthy self-image and are contrary to God's Word:

- **Feeling bad is the result of not being good enough.**

Whether it stems from the people you esteem and see in a positive light or from the reward system we've learned during childhood, it is quite easy for us to assume when we feel rotten or endure rotten circumstances, it is because we don't deserve any better.

We live in a society where we epitomize people who seem to have "good results". While I was in a destructive relationship feeling unloved, underappreciated and taken for granted, I felt there was something that I wasn't being. As "good" as I thought I was for him, I beat myself up for not being better, not being prettier, because if I were, he wouldn't treat me this way. I began to look up to women who appeared to have the result that I wanted. In some way they had mastered being something I was aspiring to be. And the gauge was their left hand. Whether I was in a supermarket or an airport; driving on the freeway or walking down the street. I saw every woman who wore a wedding ring as "accomplished". There were times I would stare and say out loud, "someone loves her". I would ask myself, "HOW did she become a woman someone loves?".

Here I was in a relationship grasping for straws, trying to retain his love when I was merely on retention. And I saw these wives and fiancés as women who had succeeded at becoming what I was failing to be. They were valuable, indispensable and a picture of every way that I was failing. I would look and wonder how their personality may be different, in what ways they looked better, spoke better, cooked better, WERE better. The key word here is *better*. My assumption was that because they had this result, they were better than I was. It didn't dawn on me the only thing *better* was probably their choice in men.

- **A God capable of changing this hasn't done so because on some level I deserve it.**

How many times have you sought God for an outcome which, based on His Word, you KNOW He is capable of, but has concluded He just isn't willing to perform? So many times I decided that since God is good, yet He isn't shedding goodness on my situation, I must be bad and deserving of what I am experiencing. What a self-deprecating thought! No matter what you experience, you have no right to oppose what God says about you. There are bad things that happen to good people. There are also bad decisions that good people make which yield uncomfortable circumstances. *It doesn't mean you deserve it.* Mercy hasn't allowed us to get what we really deserve. We must be honest about what got us where we are. It takes asking yourself if it was honestly beyond your control. And if it wasn't, one of the wonderful things about our loving Father is that all it takes is repentance to get you back into right standing. (1 John 1:9) And with His forgiveness, we can throw the notion of "deserving it" out of the window!

- **There's a test I failed along the way and this is my punishment.**

So often when we've made a mistake we imagine God sitting in Heaven with his arms crossed enjoying the fact we're suffering. This just isn't true and it isn't the way that He demonstrates love. He gives us His word as a guide and He sends warnings because He wants us to avoid the mistake. Instead of imagining Him punishing you for not behaving perfectly, imagine Him cheering you on in the face of temptation and yelling to you that you can make it! When you have made a poor decision, imagine Him crying *with* you—wishing with you that you had done better. We serve a God that wants the absolute best for us all of the time. There is never a lapse in His love for us; nor is there ever a time He enjoys delaying or withholding anything from us. He wants us to pass, which is why He gives an open book test!

- **My disobedience/mistake, has marked me forever.**

Many of us who have endured the fight for our lives have come out with battle wounds or scars. Battle wounds take many forms and can be emotional, internal, physical, and even social. Many times we are riddled with guilt because of the aftermath or the cost associated with a bad decision. Some of us wear the shame of a divorce because of infidelity or simply a wrong choice. There are women that have trouble conceiving or carrying a baby because of the trauma to their uteruses during multiple abortions. And others who, because of abortions, endure a constant reality that they don't have children when they know they had a chance in the past. Many women live with the emotional scars and the public mark of promiscuity, and some wear the mark because of rumors. I have a friend in her early twenties who, after having been warned repeatedly by her parents not to drink and drive, decided to drive under the influence with her sister in the car. She was in a bad collision which caused serious injuries to both of them. Over time her sister's broken bones healed, but my friend will forever have a scar on her pretty face. Even after multiple surgeries, the scar is there—it is faint, but there. And each time she looks in the mirror, it is a reminder of her mistake in judgment.

With regard to this flawed belief, one change can completely alter our ability to be adversely affected. What used to torment you can actually become a non-factor. The change is *perspective*. What could have killed you didn't. What the enemy designed to ruin your future, drove you to the arms of a loving Father. There are always consequences of our choices, but thanks be to God that He has the final say. If we make up our minds to use everything we have endured, everything we know, to the glory of God, then our scar or mark can become the testimony that saves someone else's life or future. For my friend, what was a scar on her face could have been a grave for someone else—even an innocent bystander if she had never told her story. Because a woman who has experienced abortion shares her story, the expectant mother of a prophet, president, fireman, policeman or bystander who could save someone's life, will decide to have her child. When we decide to use our testimonies for the glory of God, wonderful things happen and the enemy is defeated.

We must remember that no matter how we are misunderstood or inappropriately labeled, only that which is in agreement with what God speaks about us is the truth. And we must elevate our faith to a place where we no longer allow the enemy to speak a period where God places a comma!

- **More is required of me, but less will be given to me.**

How many times have I been in the gutter of self-pity and spoken this lie over my life? I would look at how hard I was trying to be "good", how much fun everyone else seemed to be having and how increasingly difficult or unhappy my life seemed to be. I would grudgingly make sacrifices I didn't see others my age make. Often in church we hear the adage, "you can't beat God giving!" and it is true. We aren't capable of giving God more than He will give us. And at our very best, our righteousness is as filthy rags. (Isaiah 64:6)

It is so important that we never allow the enemy to trick us out of thankfulness. It is our responsibility to be thankful! We have to remember, and commit mentally and emotionally to the fact that "God is good all of the time and all of the time, God is good."—Oral Roberts

No matter how we fare in life, nothing we do can earn the salvation we have received. Yet simply because He is God and because He is good, like David, we must believe we will see the goodness of the Lord in the land of the living! (Psalm 27:13)

Despite the enemy's agenda for my life, and the flawed core beliefs that at one time governed my life, I am resolved that I want the abundant life Christ died for me to have. I want the mind of Christ, to be transformed to His image and walk the *prearranged paths that He established* for me (Ephesians 2:10 AMP). And what became divinely clear is that in order to attain it, my previous foundation had to be violently broken. I had to identify why, where and how it began.

# CHAPTER FIVE

# Mi Familia

*"ARE YOU SERIOUS? SHE SAID WHAT . . . ?"*

*WHEN YOU'RE TWENTY-SOMETHING* and the sting of a statement made about you burns your ears and heart, that's pretty normal. People talk. People lie . . . . okay, whatever. But when a family member is asking you what you were doing "down there" while you were in college (I went to college in southern California) and jokes that you used abortions as a means of birth control, that is a sting of betrayal on another level. I asked again, "What did you just say? Why would you say that?" Her response was, *"Mama said you were down there having all kinds of abortions."*

Why would my own grandmother say things like that? Why would she start rumors about me? How long had this been going on?

When you're dealing with the aftermath of having your uterus scraped at the age of sixteen and having done it alone, while enduring the private shame and never having a parent wrap their arms around you and tell you that you're still loved and haven't been a complete disappointment, a conversation like that can be quite unnerving. Here I was twenty-one years old; four people knew about the abortion five years before, and my grandmother wasn't one of them. For the few months I was pregnant, I always felt that she knew. She was *that* older woman in the family who

32

would always tell someone she was pregnant before the young lady even suspected it.

Over the years I marveled at her accuracy and would ask, "Mama, how did you know?" and she would always say, "I just do, it's in the eyes."

So when my turn came and I was sixteen and adamant about my parents not finding out, I would squirm when I was around her. I didn't want to look her in the eyes. And while my nose was spreading I just knew that one day she'd say something, except she never did.

That had to be one of the scariest experiences of my life. You don't know what to expect if you've never had one. I think most people would agree that during the absolute scariest moments in your life, you want your *mommy*. Is anything as reassuring as a mother's touch, your mother's hand that cradles you and makes you feel safe? If no one loves you, if everyone turns their backs on you, there is supposed to be that ONE person that tells you it WILL be alright. But she couldn't know—it would hurt her too badly. She didn't even know I had lost my virginity. And would she keep it from my dad? He CERTAINLY couldn't know. So my best friend would have to do. And she did. I was wide-awake and she held my hand the entire time.

I don't remember the rest of the night. But I remember waking up the next morning, feeling empty. It was gone. My life would be back to normal. My nose would go back to its regular size. But I would never feel regular or normal again. There was an ache, a void deep in my soul. I didn't know it would be there. And I'd learn for years to come I wouldn't know how to make it go away.

Seventeen years would pass until I would heal and really forgive myself. Until that time I thought every hurt, disappointment and heartache was somehow tied to the fact that I had failed God. During my late teens I felt ruined; during my twenties, I felt condemned; although I was religious enough to know that God had forgiven me. But by thirty I felt like I was living out a sentence. Every baby shower, bridal shower, wedding, and holiday season I remained single, felt like a punishment I had to endure as a consequence of living without conviction. I would be so angered by people who would look down on teen mothers. Even in the church when people would see a young woman as a "bad influence" or "fast", I would be so angry. I was angry because I knew that many more teens were sexually active than pregnant. Everyone doesn't get caught. Everyone doesn't get pregnant. And everyone that gets pregnant doesn't have the conviction it takes to endure public shame and have the baby. There are many like me who would "look the part" and keep the secret neatly tucked away. How fraudulent. I wanted to applaud every young woman I saw with her belly sticking out. I wanted to embrace them for having the courage to do what I could not. Fornication is sin. Abortion is sin. Pregnancy is not, because only God can do that. It took years to get there.

So, as a twenty-one year old college graduate, I was still living in fear that I had ruined my life; might possibly never have a child; and might disgust anyone who wanted to marry me if he knew my truth. I was not in an emotional state that would allow me to hear the words my grandmother said about me and take it lightly.

I remember thinking, even if she did KNOW about my indiscretion, why would she take lightly something that hurt me so badly? Why would she embellish and talk to others about it without coming to me? How mean it was to tell others in my family that I used it as a form of birth control. And if she said any of it out of true concern, she certainly would not have made it a point to say something to everyone except my mother. No, my mother wouldn't find out about it for some time.

I don't know if I ever trusted *Mama* after that. And I can't say our relationship ever recovered. I never confronted her. I certainly couldn't do that, not *Mama*. But I never doubted she said those things either. All the years that I heard different stories she would tell about others in our family—some I believed and knew to be true one way or another, and some I didn't believe. The slander in our family wasn't new, nor would it be the last time I would face it. It was just the first time I was the subject. It was my turn. Her death years later, illustrated to me just how well I had mastered "turning off". If someone hurt me deeply enough, there was a way I could shut them out of my heart where nothing they said or did ever mattered much again. But in order to accomplish this, I had to be willing to lose them. They had to be expendable in a sense. Because once I did this, it was as though they were dead to me.

*May 16, 2009*

*Mama's Gone . . . .*

*It had to be about 9:15pm or so on May 8, 2009. I had been at the hospital earlier. Her breathing was very shallow. It amazed me how within just three days she had become so emaciated. I remember staring at her and thinking, "if I didn't eat a morsel for three days" there is no way I'd lose THAT much weight. I guess that's what a stroke will do.*

*Everybody called her mama. More formally, she was Mama Franklin. She was my maternal grandmother, Georgia Bell Franklin. Her children, grandchildren and great grandchildren called her "mama". She was the matriarch. Even if your mother was in the room and someone called "mama", they were calling Mama Franklin. You could only get your mother's attention by directly walking up to her. Once we all came together, there was only one Mama. SHE was the mother of us all.*

*I left the hospital because the doctor said that the shallow breathing- the short snores was an indication she would be passing very soon. I didn't want to be there; not because I didn't think I'd be able to handle it. I felt no fear. I felt no anger. And the only sadness I felt stemmed from the damage of unhealthy relationships and hurts that I knew once she passed, would never be dealt with by some of the members of my family. I knew there would be a void-an abyss—a dark place that could linger for generations to come. There would be no reconciliation, and unless they really came to Jesus at some point, no healing either. My mother was there, but even still, I just knew this was one transition I didn't want to be present for. So, I made it home and had been there for a short while. I was sitting on my couch and my phone chimed. It was a text message from my mother. It simply read, "Mama's gone. She passed at about 8:00 pm this evening." I stared at the text. I stared at the series of words that reflected a permanent change. Mama's gone. It's over. I stared at my phone and heard myself say, "Mama Franklin died." I was numb. I felt for the hurt. I looked for it deep within and it wasn't there. Why can't I feel anything?*

If you never really trusted family—extended family, where do you learn to trust? And if you never really felt that you "fit in" how do you avoid spending your life searching for validation? THESE: the dysfunctional family, the betrayals, the disappointments and letdowns, are the reasons the revelation about our acceptance and justification in Christ are so life altering. [Romans 8:30-35]

*For every time I remember trying to hide my faults and cover my shame so that I could still be loved, I praise God for loving me for me. All of me—the good—the bad—the flawed.*

Again, I had to make this work.

I had to succeed at being a Christian. I had already failed on so many levels. My familial relationships were distant and weak. I knew that at Mama's funeral I would see family members I hadn't seen in years. Upon coming into the fold at twenty-one, I didn't spend much time with my extended family anymore. After college, I had stopped trying to fit in. I no longer cared to change the things they said about me. I just wanted to start over somewhere different. I knew I had never really given them reason to say I was "stuck up". I am extremely shy and growing up my shyness was always misinterpreted as "stuck up". I never felt pretty or small enough, and most of the time if I could go in corner and hide, that is what I would do. I never felt like I was ENOUGH, yet the complete opposite was the label that had been affixed to me. I have quite a few older cousins and I thought they were so "cool". The women had boyfriends and the men were attractive and fast talking. And I was reminded quite often that I didn't fit in as a Catholic school girl; a good student.

As a child, my family was entertaining. There was ALWAYS something going on at Mama's house. There was the time my uncle was stabbed outside of 7-Eleven. His story was that someone walked up and stabbed him for no reason. This is the same uncle I had to hide my purse from during visits to my grandmother's house. If I was washing dishes, I had to make sure I put my watch in my pocket or else it would have come up missing. This was also the same uncle who approached me as a child and asked me if I had any money as he pulled an ophthalmoscope out of his pocket. He had stolen it from his doctor's office and was now trying to sell it to me, a child. He kept saying, "Look, I have an eye thing . . . wanna buy it?" as he flipped his wrist with the item in hand trying to make it hold its upright position. I just remember thinking, *"you must obviously have to be a doctor to properly manage it"*. Besides, how would I explain to my parents that I had said device in my backpack? It just felt wrong. He was also the same uncle that would take me to the corner store when I was a small child and tell me he would buy absolutely anything I wanted. No matter how much candy I got, it was never enough. He had to make sure I had a soda and chips and would offer anything else. That was my uncle and I loved him. The older I got, and the more I understood life, I realized he was a drug addict and career criminal. But I grew accustomed to hiding things when he was around. It was what I had to do. It wasn't even an inconvenience. He was my uncle. Eventually though, I saw his addiction for what it was. I knew that stealing wasn't okay and I saw how much he had hurt my family.

That was my uncle.

I had another uncle, my mother's other brother. He would make cookies for us when he got off of work. He was kind. And then he went to a party as a young man, put his drink down and came back to it later. He was never the same. He would answer the phone and meow like a cat. He would laugh hysterically for no reason at all. It didn't bother me, I was used to it. We got along fine and he was nice to me. But by the time I turned sixteen he would call me a *bitch* every time I came into his presence; only me and no one else.

To this day I don't understand what happened or why he stopped liking me. We were fine and then we weren't. I acted like I didn't care, but I did. I still do. He had never done anything to me until then. I really felt sorry for him.

As a little girl in Catholic school I would envision myself laying the palm of my hands on my uncles' foreheads. I knew they needed prayer and I would ask God to have them come to me for prayer. This is ironic because since I grew up catholic, other than making the sign of the cross, I knew nothing about using my hands to pray. I knew nothing about the "laying of hands"; it was just a vision the Lord gave to me way back then.

I had an older male cousin about ten years my senior. As a pre-teen I really admired him. I thought he was cute and he had pretty girlfriends. I had a special affection for him. I now believe it was because of an inappropriate intimacy we shared when I was about three or four years old. I didn't remember the episode until I was an adult. But in trying to understand the sources of my low self-esteem, I asked the Lord to shine light on areas and relational occurrences that I had overlooked. While searching for roots, you never know what you may uncover. When I was twelve my parents allowed me to have my hair cut for eighth grade graduation. I had always had long thick hair that I wore in ponytails. I loved my new haircut. I thought it was stylish and I felt attractive. I called my aunt's house to tell my older female cousin (his sister) about my new haircut. I was BEAMING. I remember him answering the phone when I asked to speak to her. I'll never forget him asking why I wanted to speak to her. He then said, "I hope you don't think you're cute just because you got your hair cut; you have to lose weight first". I felt a knot in my throat and as the tears came to my eyes, I just said, "never mind". I no longer wanted to speak to her, because now, I knew he thought I was fat and ugly. I didn't care about my haircut. I just wanted to disappear. Often times I look at pictures of myself and remember how unhappy I was at the time, with my size and the way I looked in general. No matter what, I have never been small enough to feel good about myself.

Over the years, layers of concrete were poured on top of that core belief. The one time I actually felt pretty, a person whose opinion really mattered, slashed my confidence. Some things we never recover from unless God supernaturally delivers us.

I'm a sensitive person. I now understand that it is part of my spiritual makeup. With a tremendous burden for prayer, I can sit next to someone and feel their hurt or emotional pain. It is as if I absorb energy and moods. And whatever I feel, I feel at concentrated levels. I used to think that the gift was a curse and when misappropriated or not properly managed, it can be. I've always longed to see people in a better state; thus, the reason I wanted to pray for my uncles as a child. Before I learned how to expect Jesus to be the center of my joy instead of life circumstances, I was always on edge. I was always sad. My moods were unstable and an argument or having my feelings hurt could send me into a tailspin. Neither of my parents was that sensitive and I didn't understand where it came from. I couldn't understand why things would hurt me so badly that I would feel I could no longer endure.

Finally, the time came when I understood that emotional dispositions are hereditary. By learning about my grandmother, I began to understand myself. I always say that it wasn't until my paternal grandmother died, that I *really* knew her.

I called her Mama Arceneaux. If only I had *known* her while she was alive and beyond the boundaries of a grandmother. Had I known her more as a woman and a wife, I would not have felt so alone and misunderstood. I would have better understood there was an innate trait in both of us that enabled us to yield ourselves completely to a man even when we didn't get what we deserved in return. She was shown more consideration than me for sure. My grandfather married her. Remember, I was left holding a shoebox in a driveway. Once literally, yet figuratively many times over the years that followed.

I always saw her as my grandmother. I noticed how accommodating she was to my grandfather and how much she spoiled him. But it was normal to me. It was all I knew. I don't remember her working, although I know she had a career and retired after I was born. She graduated from high school at fourteen years old (I know right?), belonged to the Delta Sigma Theta Sorority and graduated from Xavier University in New Orleans. While my maternal grandmother grew up on a farm and fed tea cakes and other sustenance to the outlaws Bonnie and Clyde, who hid out on my great-grandmother's property in Longview, Texas, my paternal grandmother was a college graduate and dedicated civil servant. There was always a silent and polite battle of two worlds. My two families were so completely different.

When Mama Arceneaux died in my arms, I was twenty years old. We shared a moment after the heart attack from which she never truly recovered. Before she was released from the hospital, she was in intensive care for quite some time. The cardiologists weren't expecting her to live, so my grandfather flew me from southern California to Fresno where the two of them had been visiting her sisters. I combed her hair and she held my hand. I stopped and we just stared at one another. There was an exchange of apologies and forgiveness without uttering a word. I just knew that we were fine. I knew that she loved me, even though she was hard on me at times. As I was growing up, I couldn't understand why she would tell me I was getting too much sun (my complexion getting too dark), and stayed on me about keeping my weight down. Now, I look in the mirror and see her. I see why she was hard on me. She looked at me and saw herself. I always thought my grandmother was beautiful and I can probably count on one hand the number of times I saw her fingernails unpainted. I never saw a grey hair on her head until after the heart attack when she was no longer able to go to the salon. I knew I loved her. But I don't think I understood just how much until her funeral. I wasn't saved yet. I knew nothing about crying out to God or going to the scriptures for comfort. I just remember pleading with them to take me out. I couldn't breathe and I certainly couldn't view her in the casket. Where did all the time go?

One year and a half after Mama Arceneaux died, Granddaddy passed, and I went to spend about a week with Auntie Joann (my father's sister). To my surprise she had brown grocery bags full of letters. They were letters taken from my grandparents' basement, dated from the 1940's to the 1960's. All of the letters my grandparents wrote back and forth to one another while they were courting. And all of the letters she received from her sisters while they were young adults living in different areas. There were also letters my grandmother wrote as a young wife and mother to her sisters, but never mailed. I put every single letter in chronological order, opened and read them. I met my grandmother, the woman, Alethia Arceneaux.

I cannot tell you how many times my grandfather cheated on her during their courtship. I cannot tell you how many letters she wrote with a broken heart. Nor can I tell you how after reading all of the letters about all of the cheating, I still managed to enter a relationship that duplicated that. It's insane when I think about it.

But now I understand that I never got to see fidelity up close and personal. Every marriage in my family had suffered broken vows. As a child I may not have known why the marriages were suffering, just that they were suffering. What I always found familiar was an imbalance of power and the wives overcompensating and not being duly considered. I saw married men in my family flirt and I saw their wives hurt as a result; all of them. And it all brings me back to my feet being firmly planted and the concrete of core beliefs being poured slowly but surely around and over me, leaving me with nowhere different to go.

I spoke to Auntie Joann about the letters. She hadn't read them and had no desire to. She told me she had lived it and she remembered well the experience. As a child and teen, she was well aware of her father's indiscretions. She told me about a time that he was dressing to go out with another woman and my grandmother was begging him not to leave. He ignored her and went to his car. Crying and begging she grabbed the door handle. He began to drive down the street as my grandmother clung to the door handle. She was dragged on the ground as the flesh ripped from her legs and blood spewed onto the asphalt. She couldn't or wouldn't let go. The pain of asphalt ripping her flesh was easier for her to bear than the pain of waiting that night until her husband returned home. My aunt told me my grandmother limped into the house, her legs dripping of blood and torn tissue. As my aunt cleaned her mother's wounds, she felt she was cleaning a mess her father made. I was infuriated by the story and Auntie Joann told me she was angry having lived the story for too long.

There was always an undercurrent that fueled a distance between my granddaddy and me. I overheard something that changed everything. Don't get me wrong, he was nice to me, bought all four of us grandkids GREAT gifts all of our lives. We were treated to vacations, summer camps, and our grandparents spent time with us. Granddaddy even picked me up from school everyday and I got a two-dollar allowance each Friday (which I usually spent buying press-on nails). They were actually model grandparents. But my grandfather always told me I had a heart of stone. He said I was *cold*. Me, the same little girl whose practice of making the sign of the cross while watching wild animals shows with them, got his attention? He would say to my grandmother, "she sure does pray a lot". I would constantly pray for the prey. I remember the night he tapped my grandmother because I kept making the sign of the cross. I was catholic and it was the only way I knew how to pray at the time. So, with that in mind, I couldn't understand how he thought that I had a heart of stone.

It was not until much later as a teen that I understood it was because I wasn't like my brother and two cousins. I didn't sit on his lap and cling to him as most children do their grandfathers. What he didn't know was that it had something to do with what I overheard one day while he and Mama Arceneaux entertained company. I was playing in the dining room, which was right outside of their kitchen when a lady caught a glimpse of me through the doorway. She asked, "Oh, is that her? Is that your beautiful little granddaughter you always talk about?" I heard him say, "No, that's the other one." I didn't go home and tell my parents. I just kept it to myself. I just felt like I knew how he REALLY felt about me.

I have a cousin, Kaila, Auntie Joann's daughter. We are four months apart and she is who he referred to as his *pretty yellow girl*. Since she was his *pretty yellow girl*, I never quite understood where that left me. So, when he said I had a heart of stone, I just looked at him. It didn't offend me at all, because I knew he had never known I had overheard him. I also knew I wasn't pretty enough or light enough in his eyes. I wasn't his *pretty yellow girl*. If only we understood how our words birth insecurities in others.

*A foundational layer of concrete poured—I wasn't pretty enough.*

I don't think my perception of him changed after I read the letters, yet the letters enabled me to see them as people, regular people off of the pedestal that Mama Arceneaux and Granddaddy sat on. My grandmother wanted her beau to be faithful. After marriage, she wanted her husband to be faithful. She wanted to be enough for him. She wanted to be able to trust him. She wanted her husband to herself. And she wanted to be happy. How many of us can relate? How many of us have or are waiting on the actions of someone else to make us "happy"? How dangerous. We are leaving how we feel, even about ourselves, in the hands of someone else. My grandmother was a devout catholic, but how I wish I could reach back to that young woman and minister to her the love Christ has for her about her worth; tell her how beautiful and talented she was; and how she deserved someone who cherished those qualities about her enough to be loyal. But I guess if I had gotten to her, she may not have married my grandfather and I wouldn't exist; an interesting twist.

Wow, life is funny like that.

Obviously, I cannot minister to that young lady; but I can minister to myself and to young women in similar predicaments and explain that who a person is, they just are, and unless they have a *come to Jesus* moment, you can count on them being the same. We must understand that when we marry, we marry what IS. To marry mere potential is dangerous. The heartache I read about in my grandmother's letters dated during the 1940's was the same heartache I read about in the letters dated two decades later. It was a heartache that made her want to take her life. It was the same heartache that caused her heart to eventually stop beating.

Even wives have to be careful about misappropriating affections towards their husbands. We aren't to love anyone or anything more than we love Christ. Part of loving Christ and being loyal to Him, is loving what He wants for us. I told a heartbroken wife once that what she thought was love had been idolatry. Her husband had become her god, and everything else, including God had taken a backseat.

That my love, is *dangerous* territory. When you are hopeless in the absence of a person's love, your hope is no longer in Christ. And He is the only one worthy of such emotional dependence. When Jesus is on the throne of your heart, you won't sacrifice your emotional or physical health for the sake of anyone else's validation or acceptance of you. You will know your worth and understand with *divine clarity,* that you have already been accepted by the *beloved.* When you worship the man who took thirty-nine stripes and allowed himself to be nailed to a cross for you, then a man who cannot tell the truth or treat you well will NOT impress you nor hold your attention.

When I came home and told my father about the letters, he told me I shouldn't have read them—that they were personal, and only the business of the addressors and addressees. I said, "But daddy, they're dead. Besides, I didn't read them for entertainment, but to better understand my grandparents." And I'm so glad I did. Reading about my grandmother allowed me to understand my own proclivities and my natural bend towards depression. I can thank God now for SUPERnatural deliverance. My father told me he remembered no affairs and that my aunt had a vivid imagination. But I had read the proof and I understood there were just some truths my father wasn't willing or capable of accepting about his parents. If my father were alive today, I cannot say this chapter would exist.

Someone has to be willing to share their experiences and sacrifice "image" so others will know that they aren't alone in their sufferings, thoughts and temptations. The world revolves around pride and egos, but in the kingdom of God we comfort one another with the same comfort we have been comforted. (2 Cor. 1:3-4). We share our experiences to create a bridge for someone else to walk over the troubled waters that their predecessors narrowly escaped. If I can share something with you that will help you not to lose as much time trying to stay afloat, you will be able to cover more ground—more territory for the kingdom of God. If I learned a path through a battle, I should provide you a roadmap out, just as Christ has for us.

The women on my mother's side of the family (with the exception of my mother) broke hearts instead of having their hearts broken. And they ALWAYS had a man around when they wanted one. They related to men very differently.

I didn't get that gene. No, seriously, their "man handling" habits aren't the ones I gravitated towards or "picked up". Perhaps it was because my mother was so different than her mother and sisters, and the dynamic between my parents in my home actually resembled that of my paternal grandparents. On the other hand, I was never able to intently study or observe my maternal grandparents' marriage, because my maternal grandfather, "Pa-Pa", died when I was three. The few memories I have of his and my grandmother's interaction actually substantiate the relational tendencies and instabilities on my mother's side of the family. To this day, on my mother's side of the family, the women are in charge of their homes and all that goes on therein.

## CHAPTER SIX

# ALL Exposed

HAVE YOU EVER thought one way about a thing only to find out it isn't at all the way you perceived it to be?

One example would be when you feel you have a faithful lover, only to stumble upon information that reveals they aren't faithful at all. I am in my mid-thirties and I am asked ALL OF THE TIME why I am not married. My short answer is that I haven't been "found" yet. Here, I can add to that fact that I have always found out about the indiscretions of someone with whom I've been in a relationship. I guess it is a good thing, but at the same time it leaves me with the painful reality that in my entire life, I've only had one boyfriend that didn't cheat on me. This painful realization prompted me to shut down in the relationship department until I could figure out how and why I kept attracting and manifesting disloyal beaus.

Perhaps, that is also part of the reason I put up with so much from the *Caldecott Preacher*—yes, we'll call him that.

Albeit, he was confused, (or maybe just disobedient, only God knows) but at some point he had told me he knew I was his wife, the wife GOD wanted for him. I was holding on with all of my *simple-minded* might.

I wasn't attracted to him at first. He wasn't my "type" and we had been such good friends for so long. I actually liked his brother when I was fifteen. I wasn't allowed to have a boyfriend back then, so his brother had stopped talking to me and found interest in someone more accessible. His relationship with the young lady lasted into adulthood.

I had been friends with the *Caldecott Preacher* since I was thirteen, a freshman in high school. I always looked up to him as a "big brother" and that was the trajectory of our friendship until I was twenty-three and aiming to transform into a *Christian* woman, which meant I needed to be with a *Christian* man and form a *Christian* relationship, although I had no idea what that looked like at the time. I had a very simplistic idea of Christian relationships. I thought that once God revealed your mate, the two of you court, marry and have a wonderful life. Perhaps that is the blueprint; just not a common enough occurrence in this contemporary age. I believe people who are dedicated to a life in Christ may have the experience, but carnal Christians go about it a completely different way.

Upon salvation, I had just graduated from college and come out of a series of disappointing relationships. I've never been outgoing enough to date a lot of people, but the few that I did date, I chose very intently, thus they were quite meaningful to me. I was back home from college for about two years before my relationship with the *Caldecott Preacher* began.

The first year, I didn't date and I became involved in church work, which was quite different and refreshing for me.

Shortly after, I was propositioned to rekindle a teen romance and that is also the period during which I had my conversion experience. It was that experience that really anchored me in Christ and for the first time, I experienced the glory of God in such a way that my flesh could hardly stand it. After that experience, there were some activities I had no desire for. I remember being in the car with *the* friend and he lit a blunt (a cigar filled with marijuana) and when he passed it to me, I declined and responded that I just couldn't do it anymore.

Something had happened to me, and it changed me. All I wanted after that was to live for God. I would now be on the quest of trying to figure out how. I told him I would no longer keep his company nor would I do the things we had been doing any longer. As I type this, I can hear the voice of Tramaine Hawkins, *"A wonderful change had come over me."*

Several months later, I began dating a young man that I was very fond of, but he wasn't Christian. We never kissed or had sex, we would just go out and enjoy one another's company. He knew that I was a Christian and I knew he wasn't. With this understanding, there were certain things he didn't do in front of me. We've lost touch, but to this day, I can say he is one of the most honest men I have ever met, and after having been lied to repeatedly, even the truths I didn't want to hear from him, were a breath of fresh air. When he was out with me and another woman called, he'd simply say he was out with *Kelsi*. And if I called while he was out with someone else, he would simply tell me he was out with her.

There were never any disappointments or misunderstandings.

There was no *drama*.

He never led me beyond where he was honestly willing to go, in the relational sense. We got along quite well. Eventually, as we had become closer he asked if I had thought about where our relationship was going. I explained that I liked him and had been enjoying his company. He told me then he knew he didn't have the influence to corrupt me, and he wasn't ready to accept Christ and come over to the side that I was on, so it was probably time that we parted ways. We remained friends and he continued to check on me and surprise me with lunch and things of that sort.

I spoke to the *Caldecott Preacher* about him quite a bit, just as the *Caldecott Preacher* would talk to me about the relationship he was in at the time. We had a strictly platonic friendship, yet he seemed to be relieved when I told him I was no longer dating the other gentleman. He would always tell me the gentleman couldn't appreciate me, and that since he wasn't a Christian, I shouldn't have been wasting my time. If only I had known at the time the gentleman who hadn't yet come to the Lord, treated me better on his worst day.

I opened up to the *Caldecott Preacher* about my dating history in college and shared my insecurities with him. I had moved back to Northern California feeling defeated in the relationship department. I might as well tell you about it.

Three men had been significant to me in college. And those same three crippled my ability to trust. The first one, I'll call *Darren*.

I met Darren at a house party. From the day I met him to the day I cursed him out, we saw one another every other day exactly. I never saw him two days in a row and I never went two days in a row without seeing him. We never kissed or had sex, he would come over, bring a blunt and we would smoke, talk and relax. We talked on the phone a lot and he seemed to be a really nice guy. I can't say I wanted to be in a relationship with him, but I did enjoy his company. I appreciated his consistency. The one time I had an urgent need, I called him and he dropped what he was doing to come to my rescue and assured me that I could call him anytime and he would come. I thought he really liked me. The way our friendship ended probably had a greater impact than the friendship itself.

I received a phone call one day from a woman asking me who I was. I was a bit of a firecracker back then, so that didn't go too well. She realized she wasn't going to get anywhere and apologized. She explained she was his girlfriend and they had a child together. She said she knew I was a friend of his, but wasn't feeling right about it and wanted to speak to me. I was *shocked*. I couldn't understand why he hadn't told me he had a girlfriend. She told me he had told her that I was fat and ugly and no one he would be interested in. I offered to meet her. She asked how often I saw him and I told her. She asked if we were having sex and I told her that we were not. I told her we had never been intimate at all. She then asked what we would do while spending time together and I told her we just talked and watched television mostly. I told her about the birthday gifts he had bought for me, and how he had come to my party. She asked about the date of my party and when I told her she explained they were both church goers and that on the night of my party, she sang in a gospel concert that was very important to her. She said he told her he had something important to do and couldn't stay. It pained her to know the "something important" was my birthday party. She began to cry and told me what I shared was worse than if I had told her we had a sexual relationship. At nineteen years old, I had to ask why. She told me it was because he would leave her at home to come and watch television with me. She said based on the dates I had given her, there were times he had left her laying in his bed confused. She said, "There were nights I was in his bed ready and willing, and he wanted to go hang out with you and do nothing?" That hurt her. By then, I understood why. His behavior was baffling to me. Still is.

Minutes later I could hear him come through her door. He asked her what was wrong and when I heard his voice I just shook my head, because I knew then she was actually telling the truth. He really was her boyfriend and the father of her child. He was in an upbeat mood and asked who she was on the phone with. I heard her say my name.

*Crickets.*

*Click.*

He called me back in front of her. I could hear her screaming and crying in the background. I just kept saying, "Wow, you have a girlfriend and I'm fat and ugly". All he kept repeating was "no."

I hung up and never heard from him again. I remember thinking, "Wow, they go to church?"

The second guy, I'll call *George*. I don't know a single woman who wouldn't have thought he was attractive. Yet, when my friends and I met him and his friends after a party, I was attracted to one of the fellows he was with. The fellow wasn't as attractive, but there was something I couldn't quite explain that I was drawn to. But George was the one who gravitated towards me, and my friends were angry about it!

For about a year we dated casually, speaking on the phone regularly. He took me out quite often and I knew all of his friends. He and his friend helped me and my mom move me from one apartment to another. We had switched cars for a week at a time, and I even spent the night at his house on occasion. I was under the impression I was a significant person in his life. I knew he had a very young daughter who I had never met, but when his phone rang, he would tell whoever was on the other end he was spending time with me. The one odd thing was that with the exception of a peck on the lips ONE TIME, he never touched me. He would greet me and leave me with a hug, but that was it. We spent time talking, laughing and enjoying one another's company. We weren't in an exclusive relationship and I didn't push, but I certainly wanted to. I knew he enjoyed me, but I didn't feel like he wanted me. I foolishly decided to love him anyway.

Late one afternoon as I was heading home from class, he called to confirm our dinner plans for the evening. I arrived home to a note on my door from a woman. Why was someone inquiring about him and why did she sign the note as his girlfriend? I was furious that someone had been bold enough to come to my apartment. I lived in a gated community, which made me even more curious. I couldn't get through the front door and to the phone fast enough. Hands trembling, heart pounding, I called her. I remember speaking to her so badly. I had a very foul mouth back then. She was very calm and apologized about her friend having left the note on my door. She explained she found the visitor's slip from my apartment complex with my apartment number in his truck and she kept it.

Her friend was a property manager for the company that managed several complexes in the area which allowed her access to enter the complex. She just wanted to know what was going on, but I wasn't hearing it. He happened to call in the middle of the dialogue to tell me he was on his way and I explained to him that he certainly was **not**, and told him who I had on the other line. He began to plead with me and promised me he was not in a relationship. I told him to prove it by speaking to us on a three-way call and he obliged. I was tired. I had been through this before.

I remember him demanding she tell me they were not together and that he had left her. She would not. She was sobbing and kept asking him why he was doing this to her. He told her he loved me and he would not lose my friendship over this. He then swore on his daughter's life he was not with her and she began screaming. I had finally had enough and told him never to call me again. I apologized to her and told her as a woman, I could feel that she was genuinely in pain, and I was exiting the situation and she wouldn't have to worry about me. All night I kept asking myself how I missed the signs AGAIN? How did I not know that he had a fiancé?

The next day she called to tell me her daughter was in ICU. We both hated the fact that he had sworn on his daughter's life to defend himself. We had a very peaceful conversation. I realized she was actually a really sweet person. I apologized again for the way I had spoken to her the day before and explained that I understood she only wanted answers. Then the strangest thing happened; she witnessed to me and invited me to church. Another strange thing happened; I accepted. Once her baby showed improvement, she picked me up one evening and took me to her mid-week service. After service she showed me the garbage bag full of all of the cards and gifts George had purchased for her over the years. Sure enough, some of the dates on the cards overlapped with the time period I was in his life. She said she had been feeling he should no longer be in her life, but didn't know how to let go. She felt God allowed this to happen so that she would have the strength to leave. After that day, we didn't speak again. But I never forgot how kind she had been to me and how the day after I cursed her, she invited me to church. She was an effective witness. A seed had been planted. And if you're wondering where George is, I have no idea. Our friendship was OVER.

Lessons learned:

- If you have a feeling something isn't right, it usually isn't.
- When you love someone, and really want to be with someone, it's amazing how you become a master at making excuses. Lies can slap you in the forehead and you can still

make a conscious decision to believe what they're saying simply because the alternative hurts too deeply.

- Think about your past relationships and how many signs you overlooked, simply because the direction of the relationship you cherished would have to change if you confronted the truth in an effort to maintain any inkling of respect. Most of the time it's much easier to make excuses and turn a blind eye to the reality that is smacking us in the face.
- If you have to call another woman, something isn't right.

While this is true, and I'm sure the young ladies knew deep inside things weren't well in their relationships, I also have to take responsibility for accepting peculiar behavior and deficient attention for so long. Even when I mentally review the details of these friendships, I realize too much of my time, attention and honesty was given to friendships that were splattered with ambiguity, and this habit I had of being so accepting and accommodating would follow me well into my future relationships. Whether a relationship is platonic or not, your time is valuable. Someone told me once, years after these episodes, that your time is your life and when someone is wasting your time, they are wasting your life. So true. Treat me like I matter. And if you like someone, there should be progress.

The third person I'll call *Greg*. Greg really got to me. Gina, my best friend in college was from Los Angeles, so most of my weekends and holidays were spent there. One weekend during my senior year, Gina's parents had a barbeque. Gina invited a young man she was dating and the young man brought Greg. I found him VERY attractive. He was about 6'5", had a chocolate complexion, glistening white teeth and the deepest voice imaginable. Barry White deep. We spent a tremendous amount of time together and I thought we were close. I remember being with him the night Princess Diana died. I dated him exclusively.

One day at my apartment, Gina and I were sitting in my living room talking with our friend Amara. I had been in the Bay Area for the weekend and had missed a party. They were filling me in on the details of the event. Amara casually mentioned that Greg had been flirting with another friend of ours, asking if he could take her out. I was crushed. Devastated is more like it. I sat there on my living room floor, feeling as if my heart had sunk into the pit of my stomach. I just couldn't understand why he would embarrass me that way. Plus, I was *really* into him. She was a friend of mine—how low. As I sat there in disbelief, I lit a blunt and decided never to accept a call from Greg again. Eventually he found out why I wasn't taking his calls and called repeatedly to apologize, but I never answered or responded. I quickly deleted the messages. A few months later, I moved back to the Bay Area.

Prior to moving, I had been struggling with the idea of going back home. I had established a new life in Los Angeles with my new family and friends. After graduation, I found an apartment in West L.A. and was searching for a job, but nothing was coming together. As the deadline was approaching to pay the deposit on my new apartment, I had received that news about Greg. I then asked God to send me a sign. I had been seeking truth and visiting churches. My mother had sent me my first bible and I asked my friend Cymetria's mother for foundational scriptures to get me started. I had a new understanding about God's willingness to direct my steps. I wanted to stay, but needed help finding a job. All I knew to do was ask for His help and His guidance. The first scripture Cymetria's mother had given me was Proverbs 3:5&6. I put it to the test.

Cymetria had just given birth to her daughter, Maya and was having her christened. A family friend flew down for the occasion and at the repast, I experienced my first prophetic encounter. After everyone in the house held hands and prayed, the man of God visiting from San Francisco, began to minister to a few individuals and I was one of them. He told me that I had been fighting moving away, but it was a move God wanted me to make. He explained that I would find joy in the will of God, and that He would put a new song in mouth. He told me that the Lord had a work for me to do. I was so astounded. I remember crying and thinking, *"me?* He wants to use *me?* I'm going to have a church home? I'm going to be happy?" I was resolved.

I went downstairs and called my mother. When I heard her voice on the other end of the line, I told her that I would be coming back home. In retrospect, I often felt that things had to fall apart with Greg. Had they not, it probably would have been a lot more difficult for me to make the decision to leave.

I left southern California feeling that there was something about me that caused men to not take me seriously and think nothing of lying to me. I daydreamed about growing closer to God, finding out more about these *"tongues"* that I had heard about, having a church family and finally fitting in somewhere.

# CHAPTER SEVEN

# The Genesis

## Empty Hands

*THERE'S A SNAKE in the bag. Don't handle the bag unless you're willing to get bit."* That's what he said. Kissing, caressing, and grinding—the night this fate I'm living was sealed. He warned me himself. Why didn't I listen? Anytime someone refers to themself as a snake, RUN. Run fast, run hard. You're running for your life, your sanity and your future. RUN!

I didn't run. That night was the first of many to come. That night was the first night that marked the beginning of bliss and betrayal, hope and humiliation. It was the beginning of a bad ending. To date, not walking away from that "bag" was the single worst decision of my life. I was 23 years old. It was September of 1999. I didn't get free, come to myself and get out of his clutches until I was 30 years old. Even after that, he influenced my life. He influenced people against me. He lied on me, he talked about me. I walked away with a butchered uterus, no marriage, no children, not even fond memories of a relationship.

I look back at having loved a man more than I thought humanly possible with absolutely NOTHING to show for it. I remember looking at my palms one day, my open hands and wondering, "What happened to my life? What happened to my twenties?"

I gave him EVERYTHING, yet walked away with nothing. With no one to hold but me, here it is, time to start over, but not from the beginning. No, I was further back than the beginning. I was walking away, only a portion of the person I brought to the relationship. It was time to rebuild, find some self worth and learn how to love—learn how to love, MYSELF. I hated him. I hated him for being my best friend, knowing all of my secrets, my insecurities and fears, dragging me on the bottom of his shoe for years and never finding it in his heart to love me. We didn't have to make it. It didn't have to work, but could you have AT LEAST loved me?

Our ending was my beginning. And what a long beginning it was. One sentiment I shared and understood though, "Free at last, free at last, thank God ALMIGHTY, I'm free at last!!!"

I remember feeling a hand shaking my shoulder. I was alive. Three hours before, when I was wheeled into the operating room, I began to shake. It was cold in there, everything was silver and I wondered, *"after all of this, what if I don't make it? What if I die?"*

I was finally having the fibroid tumors removed and I knew it was a risky procedure, because of the size of one of them. A hysterectomy was the standard operating procedure, but I asked Dr. Gentry to try her best to save my uterus. I hadn't had children yet, and I still wanted the opportunity to do so.

When I felt the hand on my shoulder, I didn't know the outcome, but I at least knew I hadn't bled to death. I had survived the surgery.

Her words were music to my ears, "Kelsi, I got all of it and I was able to save your uterus. I had extra blood on hand thinking you would bleed really badly, but it went fine. You're fine. Get some rest, and someone will be in shortly to take you to your room."

*Thank you Jesus!* I knew that moving forward I would be a lot more careful with my body, my womb. God had given me a second chance.

It took eight weeks for me to recover. A *lot* of internal healing was necessary. My womb had been taken apart and put back together. While I healed internally, I began to heal *internally*. During prayer,

Holy Spirit revealed to me that women are incubators. When we don't cast our cares to God, when we don't avail ourselves to Him to be healed, we can incubate pain, rejection, insecurities and the like, just as we can incubate a growing baby. That is just what I had done. What could not be explained in the natural was now revealed in the spirit realm. A team of doctors couldn't understand why one of my tumors grew at such an exponential rate. Hormone injections that shrink tumors had the opposite effect on mine. Something else was involved; they just didn't know what; that's because the problem wasn't scientific in nature. After my recovery, and a few weeks after I had returned to church, the *Caldecott Preacher* and I crossed paths at the vending machine. I politely spoke and he asked if he could have a few words. I obliged.

He apologized and explained that during my time away, the Lord had revealed to him that he was the source of pain that led to the health problems I was having. He told me he was aware that I had a lot of hurt trapped inside of me and that it was the reason for the growths. "I'm really sorry," he said. It was 2007, and it was my confirmation, and all I wanted was to forgive. I wanted nothing from the experience left inside of me; no residue from the years prior. Nothing.

For years I had been part of a love triangle where my esteem was slaughtered. I really believed at the time I was in the right place, but doing and experiencing the wrong thing. I thought I was in the relationship I was supposed to be in, but feeling a pain, and fighting a fight that shouldn't have existed. I didn't understand the concept of *contamination*. No matter how "godly" the initial plan or revelations, once fornication, deceit, manipulation, contention, strife, become involved, the circumstance can in no way be Christ like. We too often forget that He is a holy God. And He requires holiness from us (1 Peter 1:15:16). Holiness is His standard.

It is absolutely essential that when we come to Christ, we yield to the process of discipleship. If you don't cultivate a prayer life, expect negative consequences. If you don't become acquainted with the word of God, you can expect negative consequences. It isn't enough to attend church, sing praise and worship, listen to gospel music in your car and sit in the front row. Those things are good, but they aren't enough for you to cultivate intimate relationship with your King. You must become intimately acquainted with God and His attributes. When you know His attributes and His standards, you know when something doesn't reflect His character. I cannot stress how important it is to know when something or someone in church, doesn't reflect His character or will concerning your life. There are some circumstances that don't necessitate a revelation, just a good understanding of scripture. Many of us have been damaged and caused lots of damage simply because we didn't know any better—even worse, the knowledge was available. (Hosea 4:6)

There was a time when I didn't see the *Caldecott Preacher* as anything more than a friend. As I stated earlier, we had a strictly platonic friendship and I was fine with that. One evening, a member of his family who was known to have prophetic insight, mentioned to me that they had a dream I was marrying him. I thought that it was bizarre to say the least and I didn't give it much thought initially. A couple of weeks later, he asked me if the family member had mentioned the dream to me and I expressed they had. He then asked what I thought about it and I explained that I hadn't given it much thought at all. He proceeded to tell me that it had been on his mind since it was shared with him.

### Timing is Everything

At the time that this dream had been shared with me, I had only been saved for a little over a year. If I screamed to you I had NO WISDOM, I still couldn't say it loudly enough. Wisdom in me would have told him that it didn't even need to be discussed until we had prayed about whether there was anything to it. I would have also known that since he was currently committed to someone else, there was no physical or emotional space for me in his life and that what God wills, He also has the autonomy to bring to pass without untimely involvement. *Wisdom* really *is the principal thing* (Proverbs 4:7), and can save each of us from a lot of unnecessary heartache.

*The beginning of Wisdom is: Get Wisdom (skillful and godly Wisdom). [For skillful and godly Wisdom is the principal thing.] And with all you have gotten, get understanding, comprehension, and interpretation. Proverbs 4:7 AMP*

The *Caldecott Preacher* had a girlfriend for crying out loud. He was a minister who shouldn't even have been entertaining a woman that he couldn't potentially marry. Yet, with the onset of this dream, he began to neglect a relationship he had been cultivating for over a year. We shouldn't have begun to discuss or explore the possibility of us being marriage material for one another until he was no longer in his relationship. Even by the world's standards it is slimy to become involved with someone who is still in a relationship and here I am, at his house, at night. He told me that he really believed he had been with the wrong person. Could I have really believed that? I shouldn't have been there, plain and simple. The night I was bitten by the *snake in the bag*, I should have removed myself from the situation and put some distance between us as *friends*, but I didn't. As with many women, the encounter caused my emotions to spiral out of control and I found myself confused and guilt-ridden, now wanting someone who, just a few months ago, I wasn't even attracted to.

I stupidly believed I was hostage to an impossible situation. I can't even say that I loved him at the time, I just knew I had messed up big time and if we were to move on with plans to marry, this quandary could be masked and forgotten.

Soon enough, I realized they hadn't broken up. I was being treated as a dirty little secret and I allowed myself to be treated as such. My feelings were hurt. Although I knew his habits and his struggles, I never thought I would fall victim to them. I was his friend for so many years. I wasn't just some young lady he met and began to date. We had history and he knew all of my secrets, fears and insecurities. He was the person I would run to about this situation, but now he *was the situation*. I was at a complete loss. For months to come, I would sink further and further into a pit of despair. The entire church seemed to be gossiping about me. I would walk into the choir room to put on my robe and hear conversation about me trail off. I heard the giggles and the cackling. Some of the young ladies, whose allegiance was to his girlfriend, would boldly roll their eyes. I felt like I was wearing the scarlet letter. I used to have a happy church home and now I was the subject of mean gossip, cruel lies and even talk in a local beauty salon. It didn't seem as if there was anyone who wasn't talking about me and I didn't understand it. I didn't know yet that he told his girlfriend I was coming after him, and pressuring him to leave her. I was being played in the worst way; not to mention, my new life in Christ was beginning to fade. This was my new family, the place where I needed to have the security and acceptance I wasn't getting from my family. This was the new life that had to work. Remember I said earlier, if I couldn't make it work with God and in His house, I had no other options. I felt it was so unfair, because no one was angry with him. He didn't seem to be suffering at all.

I sat in my car one morning, sobbing. I couldn't figure out how I had gone from being single and carefree to now burdened and in despair. I was supposed to be growing closer to the Lord, and had decided I wanted to be involved with a Godly man but now I was in a relationship stocked with sin, shame and deceit. I sat in my car in the underground garage at work and pleaded with God to deliver me. I cried so hard and so desperately that I couldn't collect myself enough to get out and on the elevator to go upstairs to my office. I remember saying out loud, "Lord, if you don't help me TODAY, I'm not going to make it."

The day seemed to be passing slowly. My partner knew I was having a rough time, so she interviewed most of our candidates that day. I had puffy eyes and felt nothing better than downcast. At about one o' clock in the afternoon, a lady walked in. Something about her was different. She sat in the waiting room quietly and seemed to be watching me the entire time. It was so strange. Although she was looking at me, it seemed more like she was looking *through* me. Her eyes made me feel vulnerable and bare, so I kept looking away. She filled out the employment application and did her typing and software tests and again waited to be interviewed. It was my turn to interview, but again, my partner relieved me. As she interviewed with my partner, she continued to glance in my direction. We met eyes a few times, but I continued to work quietly. After her interview was over she politely commanded my attention and smiled. She then told me to have a good day. I returned the salute and then she exited the employment agency.

I found our exchange strange, just as I had her continual glances, but I was too consumed by my situation to think much of it. As my thoughts continued to wander as they had most of the day, I could feel my eyes welling up with tears and I knew the dam was about to break. I got up and left the office to go to the ladies' restroom. Ours was one suite of four on the floor and we shared the restroom with the patrons in the other offices. There was always a steady flow of people in and out of the restroom and it was pretty impossible to be in there alone. I locked myself in the stall and stood there crying. I heard the door opening and closing as people exited. I was finally alone and able to cry privately. The door opened once more, someone walked in, but never went to a stall. There was absolute silence. I was quiet and they were quiet and what broke the silence was a beautiful praise. A praise so beautiful that it drew me out of my despair and I found myself standing in my stall with my arms lifted and verbally praising God along with this stranger I could not see. I remember her having the most beautiful prayer language I had ever heard and for that moment in time, I felt no pain. My heart was no longer heavy, but filled with joy, admiration and thanksgiving for my Lord.

As our praise winded down, there was silence again. The moment was awkward to say the least. Who was out there? Was I supposed to just walk out of the stall? Then she called my name, "Kelsi?" I'm sure my eyes were as big as saucers. Who is this and how does she know me?

My thoughts danced and then she spoke again, "Kelsi, sweetheart, that was for you. You told the Lord this morning if He didn't help you, you weren't going to make it." I began to tremble, but I slowly moved my feet through the invisible wet cement and opened the door. It was HER, the lady from the office who had been staring at me. All I could utter was, "I thought you left."

She explained that she had made it back down to the lobby and was about to exit the building when the Holy Spirit told her to go back to the ninth floor because I was now in the bathroom. She said, "I took all of those tests and waited for an opportunity to be able to talk to you. He sent me all the way to Oakland for you. He told me this morning I had an assignment and I needed to go to the heart of Oakland."

"What is the heart of Oakland?" I asked.

She replied, "city hall." And my office building was directly across the street from city hall.

She proceeded to tell me that she knew about my crying in the car that morning, and about everything that I was experiencing at church. She told me it hurt the Father's heart the way they were speaking ill of me. I was so shocked, I just listened. She encouraged me and told me that I already possessed the strength to go on. I said nothing about the relationship and neither did she. After praying for me, she was gone as quickly as she had come. As for my day, it went MUCH better.

For a short while things were better. I had resolved in my mind I would continue to go to church amidst the gossip. I vowed to God that I would keep walking through that door even if I had to crawl. I actually remember saying those words to him. I distanced myself from the *Caldecott Preacher* and our relationship and was trying my best to get back to my personal normal.

Sitting at work one morning, my intercom buzzed and the receptionist told me he was on the line. "What does he want?" I thought. I picked up with the usual, "This is Kelsi . . ."

BOOM!

He hits me with, "I told my parents. I told them everything. I told them I love you, that we're going to get married and I know it's God's will for my life. I am SO sorry, but I was just confused. I had a vision this morning and now I know for sure . . . hello?"

"Yes, I'm here."

"Why aren't you saying anything? You don't sound happy."

"What am I supposed to say? I don't even know what to say? You told me before you knew we were supposed to be together," I said very irritated.

"Kelsi, this time God showed me and I'm sure. I told you that I've told my parents. And she and I are over. I had a conversation with her. It's done. Now that I KNOW for sure it's God's will, it's different."

That was a lot for me to swallow. My head was spinning and I asked if we could discuss it later when I wasn't at work. I will never forget the feeling I had when I put the receiver down. Had he just told me he wanted to marry me?

My intercom buzzed again and I assumed it was him, but the receptionist recited a name that wasn't familiar. I picked up the line and although I didn't know her name, I certainly recognized her voice. It was *her*—the lady from the restroom.

"Congratulations!" she said.

My mind went into overdrive. Okay, this is too weird. I stammered a greeting and asked what she meant, just to clarify.

She resumed, "Wasn't your husband just revealed to you? I know you are afraid and I know a lot of people won't be happy about it. They don't seem to like you very much, but this is a time for you to be prayerful about how to proceed. God's timing is everything. And you can believe the Lord revealed Himself to him just as he told you." And then as if she had a sudden revelation, she said, "Oh no! He hasn't been very kind to you either has he?"

"No", I stated.

She then explained that I would need to proceed prayerfully.

Over the next few months she spoke to me about divine will and how we always want what has been established in Heaven to manifest in our lives. As time went on, he and I began to plan and spend a lot more time together. He had asked me to trust him and not to give up on him, and I had decided to go all in. How could I not, since God had *ordained* it?

There was a particular morning that Holy Spirit revealed to me we were moving too quickly and that it was not TIME. I was *clear* that we needed to be at separate corners being cleansed and matured before any marriage was to take place. I absolutely knew that it was not time, but I proceeded anyway. *She* began to warn both of us that we were spending too much time together, that fornication would destroy everything and that we had to be sensitive to God's timing. That was my confirmation, but I was in love with him, and this was God's doing, so I didn't heed the warning. Besides, I wanted to prove to everyone that I was rightfully in this situation, because they had treated me and spoken about me so badly and finally; I was in love with the idea of being married. I just felt that the rest would fall into place.

But, all it did was fall. (Proverbs 16:18)

# CHAPTER EIGHT

# The End of My Rope and the Beginning of His

SOMEONE WHO USED to mentor me quite a bit told me once that being married was a lot like selling your soul. There's a meshing of everything that belongs to both parties, internally and externally.

Their bad temper now meshes with your calm nature, your jealous nature meshes with their friendliness. Their bitterness meshes with your kindness. You can see how if done incorrectly, the inner anguish and absence of peace one can experience in a relationship can feel like the worst experience on Earth. When she said that, it sounded bad, really bad. But now, as I reflect on the emotionally turbulent and exhausting past relationship I experienced; the pain the young ladies that confronted me in college experienced; the experiences of a host of friends and associates whose stories I know about, along with the pain they endured, I wonder how many of us have sold our souls without a wedding band? How must a woman really feel about herself when she doles out all that she has to someone who won't sacrifice beyond what is convenient? That hurts even when you're married actually. How many emotional divorces have there been when one was never even afforded the acknowledgement of a marriage? How many emotional divorces have there been within marriages?

Your Father knows your generous, nurturing and sacrificial nature, because He gave it to you. And to protect you from giving out too much too soon, and giving up too much without being taken seriously, boundaries were created in the form of holiness, that so many blatantly avoid. To protect us even more, we're given guidelines in scripture that describe what our husband's love for us should be like. If he hits you, is that him loving you like he loves himself? If he violates you, is that him loving you like he loves himself? If he disregards your pain and your feelings, is that him loving you like he loves himself? Would he disregard his own pain to bring momentary pleasure to himself? Would he gnaw off his finger in order to enjoy a sandwich? I think not!

We must think about which we don't take seriously—God, ourselves, or both. When we reflect on the marriage or relationship that nearly cost us everything, if we're honest, we can also locate the door of compromise that we overlooked along the way. There's always a door. There are always indicators and often times someone reveals their character to you through their dealings with someone else, well before they turn on you. Yet we're still surprised. It reminds me of the story about the lady who finds an injured snake on the road. She rescues the snake and nurses it back to health. Once it is well again, it bites her, injecting her with deadly venom. When she is on her deathbed she asks the snake how it could do that to her considering all she had done for it. It simply responded, "you knew I was a snake."

For so many years I felt like a victim and like something so unfair had happened to me. But eventually, I remembered him warning me about the snake in the bag. I didn't listen and I was bitten. It took years for me to come to the understanding that I wasn't a victim but a participant. It is so interesting to me how much we want God's gracious benefits without doing things His way. Many of us want to be married so badly that we don't approach relationships prayerfully, we don't wait for God to endorse the union, yet we run to Him for help when things are falling apart. We find ourselves in relationships where we refuse to abstain, when the word of God is explicit with regard to fornication. We take it upon ourselves to decide that grace should cover our indiscretions because "everyone else is doing it" or because it is too difficult and He "knows our heart".

We continuously label relationships as Godly, when His virtue has exited long ago.

Eventually we should all mature to a point where we understand that God's statutes don't limit us, but protect us. If I had backed away from the relationship when God revealed to me we were supposed to be in separate corners, we never would have been involved at the time of the *Caldecott experience*. So often our obedience would spare us pain and humiliation, we just don't trust God enough with our lives. We don't trust that He is steering us along the path for our certain good. We should never want to be in a relationship that God doesn't author, nor want to be in a marriage that He doesn't endorse. What relationships have you chosen for yourself without ever giving God the opportunity to be a willing participant? And worse, what relationship may have pleased Him in the beginning, that you ejected Him from, because you decided against doing it His way? Have you ever taken a game to someone's house to enjoy it with your friends and then they tell you can't play? Is that fair?

It's easy to believe that your situation is different—that because of one variable or another, you shouldn't have to bear the fruit of the spirit (Galatians 5:22). The truth is that sin is sin and "the wages of sin is death." Romans 6:23 There's just no way around that. How many divorces would never exist if God had been consulted and obeyed in the selection of a mate? How many abortions would be avoided if adultery and fornication weren't actions that manifested from a heart oozing with lust? And then there are those who feel they sin and "get away". No one ever gets away. There is always a day of reckoning. We cannot escape the law of the harvest. Whether it takes one month or twenty years, everyone eventually comes to terms with the harmful and sinful decisions they have made. (Galatians 6:7)

However, I do believe the grace that follows sincere repentance plays a significant role in the intensity with which you are affected by previous harmful decisions. Human intellect amazes me in that so often it is so impressive and yet so destructive. Frequently, we rationalize and justify our sinful behavior, even going as far as convincing ourselves that because "love" is involved, the sex before marriage or living together before marriage isn't sinful. People will often say that they are doing better and are happier "shacking", than some people who are married. If you told your child that stealing is wrong and then caught them stealing, how would you feel if they said, "Well, after Tommy and I decided to steal, we noticed we were laughing and playing while stealing, but while Jane and Johnny were doing chores for their merchandise, they fussed an awful lot." Wouldn't you retort, "WHO CARES? There's nothing funny about being a thief. Thieves go to JAIL."

If we really get to the heart of the matter, quite often we broadcast that our allegiance isn't to God. When we justify our sin and skate over his precepts, we are revealing that our hearts are not bent towards Him. We reveal that our comfort is more important than Him, that our convenience is more important than Him and that the other person, is more important to us than He is. The old adage is accurate, *the proof is in the puddin'*.

Righteous suffering. There are marriages that suddenly end after ten, twenty and thirty years and often times at one end of the divorce is a spouse that is baffled and heart broken. Only God knows the paths we will take. We know where we are and where we have been, but He knows where we are headed as well. When He provides a mate, He provides a person that can accommodate our present as well as our future which is hidden in Him. That doesn't mean that the person or the marriage will be perfect, but I'd much rather endure for the sake of Christ, knowing that I am equipped to handle it, and that there will be a reward for my obedience, rather than suffer simply because I made a bad decision and have no one to blame but myself. It's like solving one hundred long division math problems for extra credit, but getting no credit at all. Insane.

For years I thought I was living out a sentence. I couldn't seem to break free from the situation no matter how hard I tried. I thought that God had become a beastly creator that was requiring my misery for the choices (notice I said choices, not mistakes) I had made. I would never have thought that way had I really known Him. Had I known Him, I would have known that my pain was breaking His heart. Had I known Him, I would have understood that He was standing at attention, waiting for me to put Him back on the throne of my heart. I had dethroned him and let someone else take His seat. While I was trying with ALL of my might to break free, that was exactly the problem, I was trying with all of MY might. I was buying books, listening to tapes, traveling to conferences so that I could be *delivered*, when I was merely suffering from a heart condition that He would gladly heal.

Until you know Him, you cannot love Him, and until you love Him, you will not obey Him. I don't know a single person who isn't an atheist or agnostic who would admit to not loving God.

Most normal people who consider themselves Christians, whether they bear fruit or not, will stammer, "Of course I love God! I may not pray very often or go to church, but I love Him". Is it the passive love that you have for the great-great-great-great aunt, you've met once, that is more of a verbal expression than a sincere emotion? Is it really possible to love someone that you've never cared enough to cultivate a relationship with or is it just the polite thing to say? Don't we aim to please those that we love? Doesn't it feel good to make them smile?

The truth is that love is a commitment to be faithful and loyal. It is an action word. With that said, many of us have to really be honest about whether or not we actually love God.

*So kill (deaden, deprive of power) the evil desire lurking in your members [those animal impulses and all that is earthly in you that is employed in sin]: sexual vice, impurity, sensual appetites, unholy desires, and all greed and covetousness, for that is idolatry (the deifying of self and other created things instead of God). Colossians 3: 5 AMP*

I like the straightforwardness of that scripture, especially the reference to all that is in us that is *employed in sin*. It's like saying, *Who's the Boss?* We do what our boss tells us to do and we react to the demands and dictates of our employer. Often there is such a stark contrast between what we say we believe, and our truth that we perform. No one loves God any more than they obey Him. And many people obey and spend more time with their physical trainers than they do God, the One who gifted us with the bodies that function well enough to exercise. I have nothing against exercise; we NEED to exercise in order to be good stewards over our temples. But we must be honest about how we have prioritized our lives as well as whom we've prioritized.

Although my conversion had begun, I had very little revelation about just how much He loved me and how much He wants for me. We were predestined for royalty, yet we settle for being the "other woman" or second fiddle. Our Father remains attentive to our prayers listening attentively and with deep concern, yet we settle for the person who doesn't call back or show up on time. We take a seat and patiently wait for a flawed lover to respect us, acknowledge us, marry us or validate us, yet we won't exhibit the same patience while the One who crafted us orchestrates a divine union and weaves a beautiful life for us. We hang on to a lover's every word although they hold no power to speak anything into existence, yet we disregard our sovereign master Creator. We negligently decline the love of our authentic Lover.

If we really knew Him, would we continue to work against Him? Would we continue in our loyalty to carnal appetites that cause us to justify the ungodly acquisition of our desires? He loves us, has carved out a beautiful space in eternity for us, yet we ignore His efforts completely.

My core beliefs were so flawed, my foundation so unsure, my self-esteem so low and my craving for validation so intense, that the *Caldecott Preacher's* words became my source of hope and inspiration. Only I didn't know this until his tongue turned against me. It meant so much to me in the beginning when he built me up, that it was life altering for me when he had turned his affections and tore me down. He should never have had such power and influence. But such is the case when you misappropriate your affections and expectations. Such was the case with my grandmother's addiction to my grandfather. Familiar Territory.

I remember being at work one day at my desk, on the phone with the *Caldecott Preacher*. We were discussing the *Caldecott experience* and he told me I had no victory in my life. And because his words had meant so much, I shut down, feeling that I was at a complete LOSS. Because his words about me held more weight than God's, I completely checked out and lost my way. I had no direction, was void of my identity, engulfed in hopelessness and I didn't feel I could bear the pain of living a moment longer.

That Friday evening, I laid in my bed in a fetal position gripping a bottle of vicodin. One more day seemed like too much to bear, an hour was overwhelming, a minute too hopeless. I was down to pleading and surviving one second at a time. I felt I had made a mess of my life. Everyone at church mocked me. After convincing me to trust him, he had abandoned me and I was convinced that wearing this "scarlet letter" had destroyed any chances of me having an effective ministry. My mother walked into my room horrified by the sight of my condition. I remember her asking me repeatedly what had happened and what was wrong. I couldn't talk. I was waiting for God to rescue me somehow through death, before I took every pill in that bottle. I couldn't do it anymore—I just wanted relief.

My mother called the *Caldecott Preacher* to ask him if something had happened to upset me and he told her that he knew nothing of the sort. She pleaded with me, but I couldn't make a sound. I was completely tapped out. I had nothing else to give. My father came, asked my mother to step out. He sat on the edge of my bed and burst into tears. He told me that he couldn't take seeing me in that condition and that he would do absolutely anything he could to help me through this. All I could offer was silence. My parents didn't know about what was going on with the relationship or how I was being treated at church. I hadn't shared what was happening because they weren't saved yet, and I didn't want my experience to shed a negative light on *the church*. I didn't want them to be turned off. What I realized much later was that my relationship with God needed to be fortified, and His love revealed to me again.

Hours later when I tried to get up, I didn't have the strength to stand. I dropped to my knees and prayed and I KNEW at that moment with an unprecedented certainty, that if I made it past that night, it was only because God resurrected me and that I would owe Him my life and my will, COMPLETELY.

One might wonder how a person mattered so much. More than that person mattering was the fact that I didn't matter to myself enough. Although at this point, I had met Christ, over twenty years of faulty core foundation had to be broken up. I had grown up believing I wasn't good enough, wasn't important enough, and the same message from satan was being reinforced in a relationship where I was completely vulnerable, completely trusting and now completely broken. And that is exactly what the enemy wanted. Just think, I wasn't even attracted to him initially. All satan needs is a door; a door of compromise or disobedience. After having an authentic encounter with God a couple of years before, I had been distracted and debilitated by a stronghold hooked securely to the foundation of my childhood.

Thank God for Tina.

# CHAPTER NINE

## Sister Tina

THAT'S WHAT I called her. She was certainly a sister to me.

Her name was Adolphia Tina Nelum and she was one of the most loyal individuals I've ever met. Although she was old enough to be my mother, God gave her to me as a friend. She was a mentor to me and during the time that I needed it the most, she spoke *life* back into me. Whether or not I received it at the time, she still spoke positive things about the person I was, the things that I had to look forward to, and how nothing that I had endured would be in vain. She promised that one day I would be able to help someone.

As if she knew that her time with me would be limited, she would tell me things that were beyond my understanding since she was much more mature than I was. Yet she would always tell me to *put it on a shelf*, because I would need it later. And because I trusted her, I did. In more recent years, I have been amazed by just how much her advice has come to life in present circumstances. She passed away on March 4, 2005, but as I lived on, the truths she spoke to me began to unravel. As I mature, I understand more and more that God used her, not only to be a lifeline, but to prepare me for the pitfalls that would threaten me long after she was gone.

She was the first person to thoroughly minister to me about the importance of the condition of one's heart. When it came to anything that I did, she would always tell me to make sure that I knew *why* I was doing it. She would often ask me what I thought or felt about something, and quite naturally, I always wanted to give the "correct" answer, but she would continue to dig until I got down to the bare truth that I now know to be a false core belief.

I'll share an example. She told me once that she liked the way I wore my make-up, "not too much," she said. I thanked her. She then asked me if I knew why I wore it. I started off by saying that I liked it and she asked, "but why?" And for every answer I gave, she asked, "but why", until I finally admitted to her and myself that I felt ugly if I didn't wear it. I thought my eyes were small and that I looked washed out without it. She then said, "That is not a good reason to wear make-up, simply because it keeps you from having to deal with how you really feel about yourself. We need to deal with the way you feel about yourself so that you can allow the Lord to heal you." She then committed to praying with me for thirty days while I fasted from make-up. She believed that I would be able to do with or without it when we were done. I secretly hoped I wouldn't have to take any pictures during the month and agreed to the fast. It turned out that she was right. Even now, I wear it, but if I don't have time to apply it, or simply don't feel like it, then I won't.

Isn't it interesting that I never shared my insecurity about make-up with the *Caldecott Preacher*, but he would make comments that I needed to put make-up on when we were out together? Our adversary always reinforces our insecurities and self-doubt as he is very aware of them. He is "the father of lies". John 8:44 And Tina was the one who very early on, ministered to me about Ephesians 6:12. Anytime something was said or done during that time that would hurt me or upset me, she would remind me that the person was not my enemy, and that my enemy was merely influencing them. She would always say, "Never hit back. When you hit back you hit the person. Do something pleasing to God. Handle them in a godly manner. Praise the Lord. That hurts the enemy more than anything. You never want him sitting back laughing because he used one person to hurt you, and then ended up using you too." Tina certainly had a way with words.

Back in the year 2000, she spoke to me about "friendly fire". All I knew at the time was that it was a military term. She explained to me that often times in combat, when soldiers were barricaded and ducking for cover, they would have to fire quickly and under distress, often times missing their target. Sometimes they would hit someone that was on their side. Soldiers would be fighting for their lives, defending themselves against their enemies, and would end up wounded or killed by one of their own. I understood immediately why we were discussing it. I would have expected a man that was unsaved or employed by the enemy of my faith to hurt me, but I never expected it to come from a co-laborer. We were supposed to be on the same side. We were supposed to handle one another differently. I had been maimed by someone in my own camp, and being shot at close range causes more damage.

When I explained in the last chapter that I knew if I made it past *that night*, it was only because God had resurrected me; it proved true. And He sent Tina, a servant humble enough to nurse me back to life. I was just a young lady in her twenties, who had only love to offer her in return. Although we had known one another for years, our relationship deepened during the season that I needed help picking up the pieces of my crumbled life. I remember saying to her all of the time, "my life is in shambles" and she would say, "no it isn't; it just feels that way."

She became my confidant and encourager. She explained to me that her divine assignment was to help me through this part of my life and ensure that I felt the love that I needed to carry on. She told me by God's design, she had to protect the call on my life and the work I would do. She never judged me; she didn't have to; mostly everyone else did. She constantly reassured me that the season WOULD pass. There were many nights she would call because she felt a burden for me and knew I was hurting and she would say, "I know you may not want to talk and that is fine. Just cry and I'll sit here, listen and pray. I'm here."

I would cry so often because his behavior was overlooked and sadly, sometimes condoned. He was more "popular" and in a position of leadership. And when people are broken, insecure and seeking acceptance and validation in the *church* just as I was, they tend to take the side of the leader. It takes a mature person, walking in integrity to have an allegiance to principles instead of a personality. She would always tell me that when you know better, it is required of you to do better. I had been isolated and abandoned by many, but Tina constantly reminded me that I was her assignment. She had been assigned to care about ME, be concerned about ME and tend to ME. And for that I am thankful. She had picked up who others threw away.

Because of her Godly influence, I always ask God to reveal to me my motives because I desire to do what is right for the right reason; otherwise, it isn't right at all.

Tina taught my final lesson through her death. She taught me to keep my word to the best of my ability, even when it feels inconvenient to do so. It takes sacrifice, but sacrifice is the very crux of the Christian walk isn't it?

As I was leaving choir rehearsal one Thursday night, she stood on the church steps and told me to call her because she could tell I was down. She told me she missed me and had been thinking about me. I told her I would call her the next day. She made me promise. I didn't call Friday. She died Friday night. For a long time, I was tormented by the fact that after all she had done for me, our last interaction was sealed by me breaking a promise to her. Eventually I came to terms with the fact that she knew I loved and appreciated her. Tina completed what may have been her final assignment. She was selfless enough to do so. I thank God for Tina-Adolphia Tina Nelum that is.

# CHAPTER TEN

# Un–Christ–like in Jesus' name

WITHOUT JESUS, EVERYONE *is dysfunctional!*" That's what Mother Ann says.

Her ministerial mandate is to counsel and help people understand just how much we need God in the process of being healed from the inside out. She's as close to me as a grandmother and although I had known her for years, we were reunited in 2007 shortly after my surgery. While I was no longer heart broken, and was in a different phase of my life, I still had emotional work to do. I understood the natural and relational elements of my experience, but I hadn't really grasped the spiritual root of the problem, and to what extent I had unknowingly participated in it. I hadn't been delivered from the stronghold of fear that made me susceptible to the traps. She wasn't in my life to point fingers or place blame, but to help me understand the importance of having a heart completely yielded to God. She taught me how if any of us fail to surrender or mature, we will damage someone, including ourselves.

I had avoided fornication and frivolous dating, but not for the right reasons. I *feared* being hurt and rejected again, because I still felt unlovable and reject-*able*. That is not how God saw me, and my thinking had to be brought in line with His. There were critical aspects of my mind and thought patterns that weren't being renewed. I had to believe I was not what the *Caldecott Preacher* said about me years ago, what the enemy of my faith whispered to me, or what anyone else who sat in judgment thought about me. My challenge at that point was to authentically walk in the identity that God created for me before the foundation of the world.

I was brought back to the issue of the *heart*. I am not referring to the anthropomorphic heart that houses ventricles and arteries, but our emotional seat, the switchboard for our behaviors, filters and perceptions.

If the heart is rank, it will contaminate everything that passes through it. Here are two translations of Proverbs 4:23:

- Keep and guard your heart with all vigilance and above all that you guard, for out of it flow the springs of life.—AMP
- Keep vigilant watch over your heart; that's where life starts.—The Message

Think of yourself as a vehicle with your brain being the motor, but your heart being the gas. The gas is what fuels the motor and the motion of the car. Every issue in your life, every move that you make has to be fueled by something. This something is your heart, which is why the condition of your heart is paramount to your emotional success and life in Christ, overall. This brings us back to *motives*. We can be motivated by selfishness, fear, anger, bitterness or jealousy just to name a few examples. But what we want to motivate us in everything that we do is God's love.

I use a water filter that sits in a pitcher. When I buy a new filter, I must clean the filter before using it. If I don't, unwanted carbon residue from the filter will be in my water. As the water passes through the filter, it will pick up the particles that were never washed away and contaminate what should be filtered water. Whatever I decide to use that water for will be polluted by the same particles. If I use it for drinking water, I or someone else will drink contaminated water. If I use it for ice, my ice cubes will be contaminated. If I use it to clean, I would smear carbon particles where they don't belong.

We don't want our life decisions and choices to be contaminated, because that means our futures will be contaminated and we will contaminate those with whom we interact. So often an innocent person suffers because we are bitter, fearful or hostile as a result of a past that has nothing to do with them.

I remember one night in the early part of 2008 I was called into a meeting because the *Caldecott Preacher's* new girlfriend felt uncomfortable around me. I had made it a point to avoid both of them—how healthy was that? But by this point I didn't want to be lied on, discussed or misunderstood any longer. I just wanted peace. We were long over, but I was always weary of being associated with him. There was always a strain of some sort. I felt like no matter how many years passed, I couldn't outrun my past. I was ashamed that I had ever been involved in such a ridiculous situation and I didn't want any additional people to know about it. It seemed as if I was always antagonized, easily irritated and repeatedly tested. When it came to ministerial efforts, I was constantly scrutinized and I couldn't understand why the stench of our past hadn't completely evaporated.

Just as I feared, in the meeting I was being blamed because the young woman wanted to leave the church. I remember sitting there thinking about the trail of women he had been involved with since me; how he had married, divorced and was now dating someone else; and how I was being drawn back into *drama* that I tried my best to avoid. Mother Ann had been asked to the meeting to be a "witness". After hearing the allegations and seeing my despair, she explained that this meeting wasn't about him or the young lady and that although the enemy may have intended for it to harm me, God wanted to use it as a platform for the next phase of my healing. She told me I had been operating under a seducing spirit. I was flabbergasted. I let her finish and then I asked her how this could be since I was celibate and had been for a very long time. She then explained that it had nothing to do with sex, but the desire for love and acceptance. In the corporate world it is referred to as *quid pro quo*, "this for that". She went on to explain that I still, after all of these years, did nice things, went out of my way for others and provided assistance so that people would like me; not because it was a nice thing to do, but so that I would be accepted. I cared entirely too much about people's opinions of me. God was allowing me to be broken and disappointed over and over again, so that I could finally stop expecting vindication from people instead of looking to Him.

I cried all night.

Was it because I was lied to or lied on regarding the young lady he was seeing? No. I never did get the story straight and it no longer mattered to me. I desperately wanted to be healed. There were some tests that I never wanted to fail again. I was tired of circling this mountain!

Just as all of us crawl before we walk, all of us come to Christ riddled with the flaws of our human nature. When we are not tempered by the Holy Spirit of God, we exhibit immorality, impurity, indecency, idolatry, strife, jealousy, anger, selfishness, etc. (Galations 5:18-20).

It is a relationship with Christ that overwrites our wickedness and gives us access to a new nature. With relationship, we become new creatures. If the old nature persists, where is the relationship? It's a valid question. Growing in Christ means growing in our relationship with Him, not our gifts and talents. We are told not to conform, but to transform (Romans 12:2), and we're given the supernatural ability to do so, if we accept it. If we never yield our hearts and everything that is sick within it to Christ, we will never have the heart *of* Christ. And when we don't have the heart of Christ, we hurt others and continue to allow others to hurt us.

Leaders in the body of Christ have incredible responsibility. A portion of scripture in 1 Timothy 3:6 AMP warns against too much responsibility (in context, the office of a bishop) being given to a novice, because it is easy for a novice to be blinded by conceit and fall into condemnation. My focus here is the likelihood of a novice not being able to handle the responsibility for the souls and affairs of others. Just as natural development takes time, spiritual develop does as well. Please note that years do not automatically constitute maturity. There is a process and there are no shortcuts. Growing in Christ like character is synonymous with maturing in Christ. Haven't you noticed how often people who are around one another, act like one another?

I remember attending a Christmas program many years ago where the *Caldecott Preacher* was delivering the message. Things were so bad between us, and his behavior was very rude and hurtful. The message was so powerful that I could barely hide the shocked expression on my face. I couldn't understand how someone behaving so selfishly and deceitfully could deliver such a profound message. I realized two things that night. Firstly, no matter what the personal life of a leader is like, God will make provision for the needs of His people. The people, who come in sincere faith, will be provided what they need. Secondly, I understood clearly that gifts and callings are without repentance. Romans 11:29 Someone's ability to maneuver in their gift should never be an indication of how mature they are in Christ, how clean their walk is or the condition of their heart. We will fully know them by their fruit. Matthew 7:20 That goes for ALL of us. It can be easy to assume you are in right standing because you are still effective in ministry. But Paul warned against such assumptions.

But [like a boxer] I buffet my body [handle it roughly, discipline it by hardships] and subdue it, for fear that after proclaiming to others the Gospel and things pertaining to it, I myself should become unfit [not able to stand the test, be unapproved and rejected as a counterfeit]. 1 Corinthians 9:27

So often gifts and talents create platforms for Christians who have not been delivered, nor truly surrendered their hearts to God, and thus, catastrophe strikes. It doesn't have to mean that they are evil people or set out to cause damage, they just haven't matured into discipline. Understanding this helped me to understand how I ended up in the relationship that I did and how the *Caldecott Preacher* was capable of behaving in some of the ways that he had. Remember when I said earlier that we don't love God any more than we obey Him. (John 14:15)

It isn't unusual to hear that the church is a hospital, and it is. Can you imagine going to the hospital with one illness and acquiring a worse condition? While it is the responsibility of those that minister to walk as closely to God as possible and protect those that are under our care, it is impossible to do if we never yield to God everything that makes us harmful. We must be accountable to one another and it is just as important to be principled enough to hold one another accountable. When you succumb to *pleasing people* and being accepted, it becomes nearly impossible to stand up for what is right and scriptural. The person thirsty for validation will be an enabler, compromiser and will overlook un-Christ like behavior amongst their counterparts just to "fit in". It is not only pitiful, but also abusive when you think about it. When you were of the world, maybe if you walked into a store with a friend and they picked up something to steal, you would look the other way since your allegiance was to your friend and not the shopkeeper. But if the same thing happens while you are in Christ, you must discourage your friend from stealing, because it is wrong and you have a concern for the shopkeeper as well. Would you feel comfortable walking hand in hand with a thief? How can two walk together unless they agree? Amos 3:3

People come to Christ broken and weak, dependent on a leader until they learn to go to God for themselves and even after that, they still need support. A shepherd is a defender and protector and employs those who will also defend and protect. While new converts are broken and insecure they stay close to those who minister to them and may hang on to a leader's every word; extending a level of trust that isn't typical for them. And when betrayed, some unfortunately never recover.

I know what it feels like to come to the house of God desperate for a sense of belonging and purpose. I came to Christ feeling like a misfit. I didn't fit in with my family, and I didn't fit in when I was in the world. I had always felt out of place. I wanted to feel safe and accepted. I wanted to be somewhere where I could relax and be ME, be okay being the person I was. I needed this Christian experience to work, as I had run out of options. Anyone who is desperate is vulnerable. And anyone who is vulnerable can be seriously wounded.

When you consider that we are responsible for one another, you realize that by harming those weaker than you or more needy than you, you have not only let them down, but God who entrusted them to your care. When you really love someone, letting them down makes you feel like a dirty rotten scoundrel. What hurts them, hurts you. What concerns them, concerns you. And when they aren't present, you do for them what you know they would do if they were physically there. We are God's representation, yet so often we represent our own interests instead of the interests of the Father. Thus people suffer.

It pains me when I think about how many people know they need God, but have been turned off from church because of being hurt and how many people refuse to go to church for fear of being hurt. I know that the scandals that exist in God's houses break His heart. Aside from praying, the best we can do is offer authenticity in our Christian walk. We are the only bible some people will ever read and we are encouraged to be "living epistles read of men." 2 Corinthians 3:3

Many of us pass car accidents every day, but generally, people are not deterred from driving a car. They understand that the accident occurred as a result of driver error or some other variable, but has no bearing on their need for transportation. Yet when there is a collision of some sort at a church, they avoid church all together. It's unfortunate that they don't deem strengthening their relationship with God as important as having transportation. Ironically, He is the only one capable of transporting anyone from the path that leads to a destructive end. So we must draw them.

Maturing in Christ and allowing Him to be the source of our expectations will aide in avoiding many disappointments and heartaches. We must do our part to make the church a safe place, which means having safe people, starting with ourselves. If we don't leave the enemy anything to work with, he won't be able to go to work within us. May we want to fall so much in love with God that there is nothing inside of us that resembles the enemy—nothing that he can lay claim to. (John 14:30) How wonderful would that be! It's not enough to bear the name of Christ, we want to resemble Him as well. I am the only person responsible for my behavior and you are the only one responsible for yours. No one else.

# CHAPTER ELEVEN

## Big Girl Pants
## (or dress, I guess)

LADIES PLEASE. IF I hear one more scenario from a person who has been taught the standards of God and has sat under sound bible teaching for a sufficient amount of time, cry "WOLF" (in sheep's clothing), I am going to scream! Well, not really. I will comfort just as I have been comforted, but I will certainly tell you to accept responsibility.

The best defense against becoming prey is the sword of the spirit, which is the word of God Ephesians 6:17. If you know what the bible says about sin, no one should be able to manipulate you into thinking sin is acceptable on any level. If you know fornication is wrong, then it shouldn't matter he promised to marry you. If you know it would be wrong to sleep with your unsaved ex-boyfriend, then you also know it is wrong to sleep with an apostle, bishop, preacher, teacher, reverend, pastor, elder, deacon or anyone else if you aren't married to them. When you play on the enemy's turf, you give him access. It isn't really fair at that point to call foul because he isn't the one who trespassed, you did. What you sow in the flesh, you will reap in the flesh. Galations 6:8

My story isn't so exceptional. If you're still reading this book, then most likely you have a story as well and can relate. I know there are many women that have experienced and survived worse than what I have shared. To be honest, I wasn't the first or the last woman that was damaged by a relationship with the *Caldecott Preacher*. But what we all had in common was our unwillingness to allow the word of God to aide us in protecting ourselves.

Any time we cannot admit our fault in a situation, we haven't healed. I don't mean the false humility we exhibit when we say our only mistake was that we were too trusting or too loving. That just isn't true most of the time. Typically we just wanted to be with someone so badly, were so desperate, were so lonely, were so convinced that we couldn't do better, were so afraid to be alone, so hated spending time by ourselves, were still trying so hard to prove something to someone in our past or were so busy trying to prove to ourselves and others that we could *keep a man*, that we ignored the warning signs.

We have to be accountable and then heal the inner wo-man so that we don't make the same mistakes again. Healing is imperative. If we don't identify the root of our fears and insecurities, we can expect to experience repeat performances.

Some people are overweight because they have a slower metabolism and don't want to adjust their diet. Others are overweight because they have a poor diet and won't exercise. But for those who are overweight because they are emotional eaters, if they go on a diet and lose weight without healing the emotions that cause them to binge, they can expect to gain the weight again. It's just that simple. Emotional healing cannot be accomplished through shear willpower. It is God who has the power to deliver. And it can take time to work your way to raw emotion. Especially when you've hidden it from yourself.

You must allow yourself to absorb what has transpired. Allow yourself to grieve. Any loss, whether it's something that you needed to lose or something that was of value, give yourself time to wrap your mind around the fact that it no longer exists. I specifically remember Holy Spirit telling me one day to grieve. I had been so busy trying to cover the shame, trying to move on with my life, and trying to heal, I was denying myself the opportunity to feel pain I was too embarrassed to admit was there. I stuffed a lot of my pain deep into my soul. It has to come up in order to come out. It doesn't just go away. You may put a smile, make-up, weave or wig on top of it, but it is still there. We become wonderful actors, and actors play the role of someone else, and not their authentic selves.

Be willing to ask yourself the questions that make you uncomfortable in your own skin. Why do I remain with someone who won't commit to me? Why do I act like I don't care if we ever marry, when I actually do? Why do I tell people I don't care that he cheats as long as he comes home? Why do I accept disrespectful behavior? Why do I crave him even though he makes me cry? As badly as he makes me feel, why am I afraid he will leave? Why do I still want someone who has made it clear that he doesn't want me? Why do I feel I would be less valuable if I didn't have him? Why don't I have an identity independent of him? Why do I continue to allow myself to be an option for him when he is my priority? Those are different variations of the same question—*why don't I feel I deserve better?*

When we are finally honest with ourselves about the answer, we can ask God to reveal to us the experiences that have reinforced the erroneous thought that we are not valuable. As we begin to walk in truth and take responsibility for our choices, we no longer perceive the painful relationships as something that happened *to* us, but rather something we agreed to. We pay more attention to what preventative measures we failed to engage. Often times when women complain about their husband's behavior, the first thing I ask is, "Did you marry him like that?" In other words, I ask them if they were aware of the habit or disposition at the time that they married their husband. If so, I remind them that they are experiencing *exactly* what they signed up for and that they will have to demonstrate patience (if it is an area that really needs improvement). Sometimes we have to ask God to do a work in us, so that the situation we've already committed to in marriage, doesn't aversely affect us.

I heard a married friend of mine in ministry named Jacqueline say once, "Don't get married expecting him to change. That way, if he doesn't change, you won't be disappointed and if he does, you'll be pleasantly surprised."

As you heal, you will find that it becomes easier to be honest with yourself. You won't dishonestly label your actions and emotions. I'll provide an example. Tom breaks his engagement with Sally and returns to his ex-girlfriend four times. Each time Sally takes him back with no evidence of change in the name of *forgiveness*. She knows that if she calls it *forgiveness*, it sounds virtuous and spiritual, when the truth is that her reasons are carnal, and she is motivated by fear—a fear of losing him or of being alone. When you make a habit of being honest with yourself, you identify what you feel and what is motivating you, whether it is good, bad or indifferent.

None of us is without temptation or triggers that can cause us to digress, but there is integrity in being able to be honest with yourself and others. It's a good thing to be able to say you are wrong when you are wrong and that your perception is dysfunctional when it is dysfunctional. We will never be flawless, but we **can** be authentic.

Emotional healing also eliminates the *need* for an apology. Why do we need someone to recite to us how good we have been to them and how much we have done for them when in actuality, we know they haven't forgotten? It is because we still depend on them to make us feel validated. When they acknowledge that we were, what we already know we were, we feel a sense of relief. Consider it a convenience if you must, but don't wait for it. Don't remain in a position where you *need* it to move forward. What if the apology or validation never comes? Will you then allow yourself to be hindered because of another choice that person made that wasn't in your favor? Don't give anyone that kind of control. Keep your healing and progress between you and God, and don't yield to anyone the opportunity to interfere. As you heal, you stop pointing the finger and placing blame. Instead, you take responsibility for your past behaviors and it becomes more important that you are right vertically (with God), than right horizontally (winning the argument about who mistreated whom).

One evening I was at home minding my own business when Mother Ann called. She asked what my issue was with the *Caldecott Preacher*. I responded that there was no issue. She then asked twice if I was sure and I responded that I was. Finally, exasperated, she said, "Kelsi, the Lord wouldn't have had me call about this if there weren't an issue, so what is lingering?"

I said, "I just want him to apologize that's all. There are still so many lingering issues. I keep being pulled in to all of this. But, we're fine, we are cordial. I just feel that after all that has transpired, I deserve some type of acknowledgement!"

She answered, "Bingo. Are you willing to be held up for as long as that could take, *if* it ever comes?"

I then realized I didn't want to spend any more of my valuable time and energy tapping my foot, waiting for something that could have been the furthest thing from his mind.

I admitted to her that Holy Spirit had been impressing on my heart for me to pray for him. This had been difficult to do, so I would grudgingly spurt out the quick "Bless 'em Lord." Obviously my heart wasn't in it. And it was becoming more and more evident to me that I hadn't forgiven him. I sure had myself fooled.

That night, I got on my knees, repented and prayed. I prayed God would help me not to be irritated that I was required to pray for him. I prayed He would help me pray the way He wanted me to pray. With time, I found myself *earnestly* praying for him. I prayed that God would bless him (and I meant it) and He wouldn't withhold any good thing from him. I prayed His love would overtake him. I was so surprised that I no longer heard myself asking Him to change him or show him what he did to me. Finally, with God's help (and only with His help), I had truly forgiven. For three months I fervently prayed for the *Caldecott Preacher*. Then one Tuesday night while I was cooking dinner, I received a text from him out of the clear blue. It read, "Sis. Kelsi, I appreciate you." I put my phone back down and was shocked of course. The following Monday, he died unexpectedly.

God is so faithful. He changed my heart in preparation for his death. Had the bitterness and unforgiveness still been in my heart, there's no telling what I would have felt when he passed. Maybe I would have felt guilty, or been angry, because so much would have still been unresolved. Only God knows. I'm so thankful that wasn't the case and that when he passed, the account had been settled. And it had been settled in heaven. Selah.

## CHAPTER TWELVE

# *Who's Bullying You?*

BULLIES ARE INTIMIDATING. That is why we fear them before they ever put their hands on us. There's a confidence they *portray* that causes their victim to believe the bully is their worst nightmare. Whether that is true or not, is irrelevant, as long as the victim believes it.

I remember shortly after beginning kindergarten I went into the girl's bathroom. As I finished up, a few first graders came in and blocked my path to the door. They were taller than me and in violation of my personal space. Although a first grader isn't typically much taller than a kindergartener, I remember feeling like they were as tall as trees. When I asked them to excuse me, they wouldn't budge. After what seemed like forever, I heard the bell ring in the distance and my heart filled with anxiety. I was going to miss lining up with my class to walk back into the building and I would be in *big trouble.*

One of the girls told the other one, "She's a nickel."

I shyly rebutted, "I'm not a nickel."

She responded, "I **said** you're a nickel."

Without another word, they both departed. A nickel? That makes absolutely no sense. There was no truth to it. It was childish talk, but because I was on that level, it offended me. My point here is that we must grow out of the place where we still put stock in the things the enemy says about us. Some things he says are flat out lies meant to distract us from getting to where we are going, just as when the little girl called me a nickel. There was no truth to it and my mood was shattered for the rest of the day because of the juvenile confrontation. I was really upset. I remember going home crying to my mother that the big girls called me a nickel. My mother was quite sympathetic, at least she acted like she was. But my father was silent. When he realized I was awaiting his response he said sternly, "girl, you know you aren't a nickel."

Can you imagine that there are times that our Father wants us to talk to him about what is actually significant instead of what the enemy whispers to us to throw us off track? Can you imagine how it would feel for a loving father to know that an enemy that can do absolutely no harm to you, keeps you distracted and discouraged simply to keep you from getting somewhere you are supposed to be?

There have been some ridiculous things said to me over the years. Some of the things I have said to myself and some that others said to me, but not surprisingly, they came from the same destructive and demonic source. While the statements had no power to destroy me, I repeatedly allowed them to cause me to lose focus and doubt God. When we allow this, it becomes a vicious cycle:

Make progress → become distracted → feel defeated → backtrack → become encouraged again → Make progress . . .

As this happens over and over, we take longer and longer to get to our appointed place, until we decide that enough is enough.

Any time you decide to step out on faith, there will come the thought that you are crazy; it won't work or that you'll be embarrassed. Often times we begin to count how many times we've seen it done or known it to work for someone else. When I find that I am succumbing to the aforementioned cycle, I have to remember the promise I made to myself. I promised that when it comes to what God has spoken and what His word says is possible, I will take the chance. I would rather believe God and look foolish, than not believe Him and miss Him. It is a constant temptation. It seems that as soon as I get good at believing Him for certain things, the next set of circumstances to believe are a bit more "impossible". All we have to remember is that the enemy doesn't want us to succeed, but if we trust the word of God, and work the word of God, we cannot fail.

I remember when I believed that because of my previous relationship, I wouldn't be desirable to anyone again. I believed that my past would follow me, constantly humiliate me, and I would never break free.

As a result, I secluded myself, was afraid to meet anyone, and dreaded seeing people that knew about it. I thought everyone left my presence and talked about the humiliating situation. And for all I knew, some people may have. But I know with *clarity* who my deliverer is. And considering how terrified I used to be, it is a miracle that I am able to share it now by writing about it.

Today, I believe what God says about me more than the threats the enemy whispers to me. I am sharing with many what at one point, I was afraid to admit at all. The love I have in my heart for God's people and my desire for them to be free far surpasses my concern about what people may think of me as a result of reading about my past. Because I've been bound, I want to see others free.

People who know me know that I am an advocate for abstinence until marriage. I've been single and abstinent and have made enough mistakes to know the limits you should not push if you don't want to be overcome with temptation. My principles have sparked a lot of controversy among other Christians.

At times, I have questioned myself and wondered if I'm the only one with this conviction. I have wondered if I'll fall, or if it is all in vain. The thoughts that oppose our faith will always come. We cannot control the thoughts, but we can control our thinking. We don't have to allow the thoughts to remain. There have been times that I have been teased, as vehemently as if I were in high school. I've been told I am too spiritual and that no man would want a woman "so rigid". It has been said to me only someone with no libido would be willing to abstain. Some have said sexual temptation is natural and God would understand if we gave in at times. I have also been told the person I court prior to marriage will not be faithful if I abstain. And even worse, I was told once that my lack of consistent relational experience (due to the fact that I don't date casually) will be a turn off; since a man wants a woman who has recently been with a man so that he can feel the competition and be confident that she is desirable to other men. Since men said many of these things, I cannot say that they are untrue. But, I will say with *clarity,* the person God created me for will not have these sentiments. If my only option is a man with those opinions, I would be better off single. After all, I am not trying to be *deep,* just persuaded.

I have only been able to endure such "bullying" because of the word of God that stands up in me during these confrontations. Since I know what the word of God says, I know what God requires. When we put on the mind of Christ, we begin to love what He loves and hate what He hates, and He hates sin. He hates what sin does to us. After all I've been through, and all God has delivered me from, I would consider it an insult to Him if I were lonely for the wrong company.

My best friend, Samele always reminds me that as a single woman, waiting [for the right husband] is better than repenting and regrouping. I have decided with finality that I don't want any repeat performances, SO HELP ME GOD. I am not boasting in my own strength, because I am not capable in my own strength, but if I keep my heart subjected to the word of God, His strength will be made perfect in my weakness.

(II Corinthians 12:9)

Any time you are trying to make great strides for Christ or live a life surrendered to Him, there will always be someone who says "it doesn't take all of that," or that you don't have to take it that seriously. The enemy wants you to feel small, insignificant and doubtful. He wants to exterminate your faith and in order to accomplish this he needs you to open the door. Don't open the door. If you let him in the car, he will get behind the wheel and change the direction that you're going. We must come to a place where we love God more than we fear being different. We must love Him more than we dread our antagonist. And we must love Him enough to go with Him alone if necessary. Often times victims feel terribly about themselves because of the trepidation bullies cause them to feel. Don't beat up on yourself. Don't punish yourself or speak badly about yourself because you feel a natural reaction or emotion. When you move forward and stay focused despite feeling intimidated and doubtful, you win. You have walked in faith. You aren't defeated by your feelings of intimidation. You are defeated by your response if it is in favor of the intimidation.

It took me so long to understand this. I learned through a very rough experience that resulted in a tremendous blessing. God really does hold the power to make all things work together for our good. (Romans 8:28)

There was a season when God didn't want me to work. I had an investment that yielded some income, but not enough to live on. And all I thought about was running out of money because I wasn't working. Mother Ann continued to encourage me that everything would be fine and that I should cherish this opportunity to have uninterrupted fellowship with God. I just couldn't do it. I couldn't stop worrying about what would happen. I was concerned about what people would say about me not having a job. I even justified my fear with scripture. I would tell myself that it was impossible that He was requiring me to trust Him and live by faith because scripture says, "If anyone will not work, neither shall he eat." (II Thessalonians 3:10b)

It is hilarious to me now that I had taken the scripture completely out of context in order to torment myself. I was motivated by fear, an emotion that is ungodly. And since I didn't resist it, it had taken over. I decided that I *had* to do something. I took an assignment that provided training I needed for a lucrative position I wanted to apply for. From the day that I started, until the day that I finished three months later, I couldn't comfortably wear shoes to work. My feet and ankles swelled so badly that I had to wear Crocs. When I tried to wear regular shoes with my business casual attire, my feet would become extremely puffy and draw a lot of attention (or so I thought). They didn't hurt or anything, they were just swollen. I fasted and took natural supplements that help eliminate water retention, but nothing helped.

During the last month, I went on a business trip and they seemed to swell twice as much. I had had enough. I got on my knees in the hotel room and began praying fervently. I began to bind sickness and every work of the enemy and loose healing. But there was no anointing. I sensed in my spirit that I was in the wrong vein, so I got up, sat on the bed and began to silently pray. I asked God to reveal to me what the problem was. When I finished praying, I understood that my problem wasn't physical at all. Although it seemed strange, I knew my internal conflict was causing a physical condition. I grabbed my iPad and searched the internet with that small bit of information. He never ceases to amaze me.

The search yielded a woman named Georgie Holbrook, who has written books about emotional healing and spiritual wellness being components that can rid the body of disease. It was a long shot, but I decided to email her. Within five minutes she responded and I shared my dilemma. In short, she told me that my swollen feet were the result of my dance with the Lord being hindered and that our dance with Jesus is one of trust and joy. She told me that I did not trust Him or the path He desired for me; therefore, my feet were heavy. My body was responding to the fact that I was on the wrong path. I felt such conviction. I knew beyond a shadow of a doubt that what she shared was true. I repented and as soon as I returned home I resigned from the job. The morning after I quit, I woke up and my feet were back to normal. After being swollen for three months, they were completely normal again. I accepted that I wasn't supposed to work during that season.

I began to speak to Georgie regularly and she introduced me to the concept of false core beliefs. It was the beginning of what is now a wonderful friendship and we enjoy a mutual excitement about the Lord Jesus Christ.

The first grade bullies caused me to be late when I was supposed to be getting back in line. Don't allow your bullies to distract you. Push through and get back in line, where your teacher is waiting for you!

# CHAPTER THIRTEEN

# You Can't Change Change

KINDERGARTEN WAS A long time ago.

Recently, I thought a lot about how much I wanted to grow up when I was younger. I was in such a rush to see what life had in store, that I took for granted the things that were familiar and predictable. I didn't realize that I would long for them as an adult, because I didn't know they wouldn't survive the change I was rushing to experience.

*December 27, 2012,*

*Christmas 2012 was my first Christmas without my father. Amazing how after someone has passed from this plain, no argument seems that important. You can remember disagreements, but it doesn't really matter who was right or wrong. At least not when the love of God has penetrated your heart. When the love of God penetrates you heart, you are able to better understand a person's capacity and adjust your expectations. He was hard on me—because he loved me. He was critical—because he loved me. Those were ways that he seemed so "hard" to me, but if it was all he knew, how could he have done anything different? It was what he knew. And it's how he believed I would yield the best results. Sometimes we just have to resolve that people did their best with what they had. The thought motivates me to continually ask God to increase my capacity for Him—for His way of doing things—for His heart.*

*I lay there in bed on Christmas Eve not having shopped at all. I was just listless. It wasn't even like the pain was piercing. It almost felt like an out of body experience. The tears would fall, but I couldn't feel the emotion attached to them. I sort of felt like I was in the twilight zone.*

*But by Christmas morning, it felt like a bucket of everything that hurt had been kicked over. I thought about death. The various deaths I have grieved. I thought about my grandparents—all gone. I can still remember their phone numbers. Their houses still stand in Berkeley, CA, but other families occupy them. Other families eat there and celebrate there. And other children run around, just as we had done. It was as if our DNA had just been erased from the scene. What about all of my history? It just goes away? Their neighbors are different. All of their counterparts—the families that were neighbors to them are no longer. Even some of their children have died off, just as my father has. And I'm left with thin air. If I knocked on either of my grandparents' doors, the person who answers wouldn't even recognize me.*

*I lay in bed and looked around my room. I said out loud—where is my father? I know that he is in Heaven. But it is a reality that I have to realize over and over again. He can no longer be touched. He is no longer tangible. As if my father's presence, his fortitude, his voice, has just disappeared into thin air—exists no more.*

*I cried and this time the pain was attached. There was an ache in my heart for all of the transition that left empty places in my soul. My life was being subtracted from. And now on Christmas, it would be my mother, brother and me. Only one less, but it felt like so much more. I began to think about how dependent that made me on my mother and brother. My familiarity and security rests on the souls of these two. I haven't yet entered that phase of recreating or procreating. I have no husband or children.*

*I cried and cried. I've lost a great deal of what was familiar growing up. In these more recent years, I've had to adjust to "new normals". The church that I was born-again in, is no longer my church. I was saved there and grew there twelve years. The people I saw there multiple times per week for twelve years, I no longer see much at all. I merely hear updates or read emails. That is a loss. People who were so much a part of my pain, development and day to day activities are dead. That is a loss. Driving the same route through different seasons, seeing the same homes, pulling up to the same building, walking into the same sanctuary and smelling the same scent—it's over and that is a loss.*

*In the past three years, the landscape of my life has dramatically changed and I couldn't help but think about how our sense of security goes from what is tangible when we're younger (all of the people we love and our support systems), to what is intangible as people die and our environments change. I now hope in who I cannot see. Along the path of maturation in Christ, I began to depend on Him more and more for safety, security and reassurance; because I've come to understand that only He is certain. Everything else is subject to change. I was hurting and crying, mentally searching for everything that was familiar. Thin air. I was feeling like I was in a free fall and His will for my life was my only net. Where am I going? Where are you taking me? And I heard Holy Spirit say "Ask me for help . . ." We had a WONDERFUL exchange!!! He took my burdens and gave me joy and expectation. Not the expectation of any particular outcome, just an expectation for Him to perform in my life. And I heard, "Life is filled with swift transitions, everything to God in prayer." My Christmas gift that day—"Life is filled with swift transitions, everything to God in prayer." It's the only way I'll make it successfully and faithfully. Thank GOD for prayer. I felt better. And I got up.*

One thing about the four seasons; they change whether you are prepared or not. You can keep your swimsuit on well after summer and you can keep your overcoat on well after winter, but eventually the season will change, and you will have failed to adjust and will find yourself quite uncomfortable. I like wearing flip-flops in the summer. Flat, wedge, heeled, plain, or rhinestone, I love them. As the weather changes and people begin to transition from sandals to closed toe shoes, you may find me still trying to hang on to the flip-flops for as long as I possibly can. Eventually, the chill becomes uncomfortable and I make the transition to shoes that are more weather appropriate.

On the flip side, when it seems as if spring has been slow to come and I've grown tired of coats and boots, I will look at the brightness outside and figure the sun won the arm wrestle against the clouds for the sky, and prematurely wear something lighter. Then, feeling like a popsicle all day is my consequence for rushing the change.

Even with the seasons of our lives, we must prepare, glean as much as we can from the present moments and yield to the changes that we cannot control. Are we fair to *change*? So often we accuse it of taking too long, but when it gets here, we complain that it makes us uncomfortable.

I often refer to my toughest (to date) season of spiritual development and the beginning of my process of restoration, as my *boot camp*. For ten years, I endured, cried, prayed, pleaded with God, threw temper tantrums and pouted because I wanted a particular change. I knew that I had to endure hardness, but I didn't understand why. It was *killing* me and that was the purpose. My flesh, my agenda, my will must continue to die so that He can accomplish through me, His will for my life. I was pressed, pounded, and tested until I became so dependent on God that I released the burdens to Him. By the time the change came, my focus had changed and the challenges that seemed so prevalent and overwhelming before, no longer had the power or influence to affect me. In the end, one of the lessons I took from that experience was to always embrace what is good for the while, because once change comes and the circumstances cease to exist, the good that was associated with it will too.

Imagine having a job that you absolutely hate. The supervisor picks on you, you don't like the location of your desk and your work isn't challenging. However, you have fantastic co-workers, the commute is easy and you enjoy free underground parking. For five years you endure the supervisor's rudeness, and dream of the day you will be promoted to a position that will cultivate professional growth. Eventually, you are promoted to a better position than you expected, but you must work at a different location. You are ecstatic because change has come. Yet you realize that you no longer have the benefit of seeing everyday, the co-workers you had befriended. You now have to pay for parking and twenty minutes is added to your commute, which means you must start your day earlier. You still consider the promotion a blessing, but you wish you had taken the time to enjoy the things that made the last job easier to endure. You realize that if you had known when it would end, you would have made the best of the time with your friends. You would have laughed with them more and *lived in the moment* instead of spending so much time complaining about the position. You would have made sure to have a conversation with the parking attendant that waved to you everyday, but you were always in a rush, so you didn't. Nor did you ever take the time to savor the scenery on the commute that you enjoyed.

There is always a reason to be thankful. And you never know what conveniences you will have to sacrifice once change comes. We *must* make it a habit to embrace the good in every moment.

We should take the time to enjoy and appreciate what is good about where we are, because when the season changes, some things, circumstances and people won't come with us. And we can find ourselves in danger of being ungrateful for the deliverance we have yearned for and been provided.

We often hear the cliché, "When one door closes, another one opens." No one told me that the next door doesn't necessarily open immediately. Sometimes we have to walk through a corridor or a hallway to get to the next door. And from the hallway, it doesn't always look like it is open. Quite honestly, sometimes the hallway feels too long.!

Life can be very dirty. There are divorces, deaths, miscarriages, and failures, among other things. There are circumstances that stain and burden us, leaving us in need of being refreshed and restored.

As we walk the difficult terrain of life, we weather these storms that make our traveling shoes dirty. Sometimes to avoid tracking the debris from our past into our new territory, we have to walk for a while—away from the messiness. The hallway is a place where the mud falls from your shoes. Even as it rains in the hallway, your shoes are being rinsed clean and you are being refreshed. You have time to contemplate and reevaluate, before possessing the new territory that exists beyond the door of opportunity. Unfortunately, the mystery of the hallway presents an opportunity to doubt the same God who delivered you from the grips of your past.

I had embraced the change that I waited ten years for. I was certain that God delivered me, but when I didn't have access to the *big picture* of my new beginning I became anxious, doubtful and began to complain. In prayer one day Holy Spirit told me I was behaving as the children of Israel. I was offended by the comparison. But I went to the bible to read the story of their deliverance again and I saw the similarity.

After being delivered from the Egyptians, even seeing God supernaturally part the Red Sea, they became disgruntled on their journey. God was faithfully leading them with a cloud of His glory by day and fire by night. He was providing fresh manna from heaven every day, loaded with the nutritional benefits necessary to keep them energized enough to travel. And they had the audacity to speak fondly of the provisions they had while in bondage, as if those provisions were better than the manna falling fresh from the sky daily.

*And the mixed multitude that was among them lusted exceedingly: and the children of Israel also wept again, and said, Who shall give us flesh to eat? We remember the fish, which we did eat in Egypt for nought; the cucumbers and the melons, and the leeks and the onions, and the garlic: but now our soul is dried away; there is nothing at all save this manna to look upon.* Numbers 11:4-6

Holy Spirit told me to replace the word manna with the word *miracle*. Do I not sound ungrateful? I saw how I had been supernaturally sustained during the most difficult part of my life, and was now being led by God to whatever He had prepared, and all I could say was, *"all I have before me is this miracle."* It is a miracle. Who complains about a miracle? Oh, me. How dare we look back and compare finally being liberated with the convenience of an assigned parking space, the comfort of a routine or the familiarity you relished? How can any of that be compared to being more intimately acquainted with God as a deliverer? Shouldn't we trust Him enough to know that He didn't deliver us to abandon us? Though insane, we can be tempted to miss what we do *not* miss.

We can live without regret if we maximize our opportunities, nurture our relationships and do the best that we can with the moments we are given. Even when we don't have the best start, we can seek the Lord about how to finish well. We can leave a mark and create the building blocks for cherished memories. When we maximize our opportunities, no matter how it ends, we won't have to bitterly long for yesteryear, because we will know we did our best and left nothing undone or miscommunicated.

Whether we're ready or not, time *will* move forward. And we will find awaiting us in new territories and domains, and disguised as challenges, new opportunities to grow and trust God. Hopefully as we reminisce about each past victory, we will realize that not only are we equipped for what lies ahead, but that we know Him, trust Him and love Him more than we did before. I don't want to limit God. I want to live with the confidence that He will always trump the enemy's plans for me, present a gain from every loss, and guarantee that every delayed blessing will be well worth the wait. That is my prayer.

"Life is filled with swift transitions, EVERYTHING to God in prayer."

## CHAPTER FOURTEEN

# Clear Perspective

I REMEMBER BEING in a church service one evening. The music was blaring and as I looked around, everyone was praising God. I was pensive. My feelings reflected a mix of gratitude and guilt. I really believed God was good and that gave me joy.

Yet, I couldn't ignore how badly I felt. I remember wondering that night, "If God is so good, why do I *feel* so badly?"

For the most part, during that period in my life I had a very sad countenance. Many days I carried burdens that I wouldn't wish on my worst enemy. Often times we say things like, "If I were more selfish, I would take better care of myself." But perhaps the truth is that if you cared more about yourself, if you loved yourself more, you would be more selfish. I don't mean selfish in the self-serving or self-pleasuring sense, but in a way that would cause you to be more protective of yourself. The better you are, the better you are for everyone that you impact. If I had a Maserati, I wouldn't allow anyone to mishandle it, drive it recklessly or trash the interior. It is a fine automobile that is very valuable. And because I would respect its value, I would require that others, who want to enjoy it, do the same. I used the Maserati as an example, but we should be just as protective of anything God entrusts to us. We shouldn't let others dictate the value of God's gifts, not even the gifts of *us*. Just as we are stewards over our homes, cars, spouses and children, we are stewards over ourselves as well, since giving ourselves to God.

Taking care of yourself and guarding your heart doesn't mean that you shut down, put walls around your heart and become distrustful. It means not giving yourself to be handled carelessly, not putting yourself in harm's way, and setting standards with regard to the way anyone interacts with you. Consider it your way of protecting God's investment in you.

That night in church, with the music blaring, I got on my knees and screamed to God as loudly as I possibly could, "HELP ME!!! PLEASE HELP ME!!!"

I was at the end of my rope, trapped and suffocating. I was in the clutches of a stronghold that I equally hated and feared being without. Similar to joining any other recovery program, I had to surrender the methods that came naturally to me, which positioned me in my current predicament, and follow a new set of rules. As I mentioned in Chapter Four, the start was acknowledging, thus chipping away at a faulty foundation.

When I was in grade school, one of my teachers let my class watch an old movie, *The Black Stallion*. In the movie, a young boy was traveling with his father on a large ship and the ship sank. The boy and the wild horse that was being transported, survived and were stranded on a deserted island. The horse hadn't been broken, and wouldn't let the boy near it at first. With time, they warmed up to one another and the boy would ride the horse along the beach, holding on to the horse's mane. The horse would run so fast, that the boy's hands would bleed. Upon being rescued, a racehorse trainer saw that the horse ran faster than any other horse he had ever seen and decided he would train it to run in races. He was quite confident that the horse would win. But because the horse wasn't broken, they couldn't saddle it, the horse wouldn't stay in its lane while running, and when the gates would open, the horse wouldn't run. The times it did run, it would stop short. It wasn't broken, and therefore, it didn't obey the trainer. Although the horse had the intrinsic ability to outrun its opponents, it lost every race due to being disqualified.

Once the horse endured the process of being broken, it stopped bucking, it didn't throw the saddle off, or run into other lanes. It started at the gun and beat every other horse. It didn't have to learn to run, because remember, the speed was already there. The horse was a champion the entire time, but this wasn't realized until it succumbed to the process.

Imagine what victories await you at the end of your process, once you fearlessly abandon the habits, mindsets and behaviors that have kept you imprisoned and circling the same mountains in different years and locations. Life has broken you, but your brokenness aides you in submitting to God's plan. Many people finally yield to God after they have done everything they can to change their lives and failed. One can become so accustomed to discomfort, that the possibility of the pain not existing is unimaginable. But it is possible. We have hope in Christ. The ride can stop so that you can get off. Peace is an option.

I cannot tell you the exact date or time that I stopped feeling the ache of the *Caldecott Experience* and was freed from the hostile clutches of what felt like repetitive defeat. I just know that I faced a new direction, kept walking and eventually looked down to a clear path and the hurt was gone. There was a time that the pain was etched so deeply into my soul, and anchored to a place so deep, that I thought it would disable me for the rest of my days. But I don't walk with a limp. And if I feel for it, no remnant of the nesting place for that person is there.

I drive through the Caldecott Tunnel all of the time without the memory of that fateful day. I mentioned in chapter one that the experience separated my life into before and after. I now see it as before my path to clarity and after my path to clarity. The experiences and relationships birthed from that experience are rich and have blessed me tremendously. I am thankful for the interruption of the regularly scheduled program that was my life. Had I continued on that path and the *Caldecott Experience* not occurred, I don't know where I would be or what would have become of my life by this point. I just know that the life I'm living is better. That experience was the catalyst that propelled me on a journey from my reality to the truth.

Upon completing this chapter, missiles of doubt and fear were launched and I began to wonder what the *religious* people would say about me sharing the details of my transgressions. Will my great aunts tell me that my grandparents' private turmoil should have been buried with them? But I remembered looking into the hollowed eyes of young ladies who grieve the loss of an innocence that they never learned how to protect. I see them afraid and lonely, thrust into the affairs of womanhood that they aren't emotionally mature enough to bear. They think no one knows, but someone who has been there knows exactly where they are. And they shouldn't feel alone.

I think back to coming into the fold at twenty-one years old, alone. No roots in this Christian culture that was so new to me and I remember how unqualified I felt. I had no Sunday School class as a child, no father in the pulpit, mother in the choir stand or grandfather as a pastor. I looked at others around me who were raised in this culture and when compared to them, I felt dirty and less than. I didn't feel I had the pedigree that I thought was necessary to be anything great in God. I thought by serving, and volunteering for any and everything, that I was earning my keep in the household of faith. I often see the same longing in the eyes of people who come to the house of God desperate for change. Who am I to withhold a testimony about God delivering me from feeling lost, desperate, hopeless and dispensable when *"Christ Jesus, who, being in the form of God, thought it not robbery to be equal with God: But made himself of no reputation, and took upon him the form of a servant, and was made in the likeness of men: And being found in fashion as a man, he humbled himself, and became obedient unto death, even the death of the cross." Phillipians 2:6-8?*

If with my life and my words, I don't make an effort to convince someone that God is real and that the *"LORD'S hand is not shortened, that it cannot save; neither his ear heavy, that it cannot hear." Isaiah 59:1 KJV,* then I have selfishly hidden the grace of God that was bestowed to me when I was desperate for what I did not know how to identify. He revealed Himself to me and changed my life. There is no better comfort, and no greater feeling, than that of His presence. He is our deliverer. We don't have to psych ourselves out, and pump ourselves up, to keep up with the routines of life while burying an emptiness that screams from within. He can change whatever you commit to His authority.

I pray that my journey has inspired and challenged you to investigate the integrity of your core beliefs; has given you the courage to release anything that hinders you from living the abundant life Christ died for you to live; and opens a floodgate of excitement that cannot be closed. And remember, if by heeding the warnings provided in this book, you can cross my bridge, you won't have to [nearly] drown in despair.

*Father, I pray that every visual witness to this testimony is encouraged, stirred and ignited to become sturdier where they are weak, resolved, where they are doubtful, and strengthened, where they are tempted. May the truth that there is nothing better than you begin to penetrate their hearts and satisfy their souls. And may there be no end to this revelation. In Jesus' name I pray, Amen.*

Transitions will continue and life will go on. The future is unknown, but a few things I know. God is good. And **Clarity is Divine**.

♥ ♥ ♥

If you don't know the Lord as your personal savior, salvation is easy. Pray this prayer and change the course of your life and eternity. Many say, "Oh I believe in God." That is good, but it isn't enough. Even demons believe, and tremble in fear of God. (James 2:19) Salvation is a relational commitment.

God, I come to you as a sinner. I am sorrowful for my transgressions. Please forgive me of all of my sins and cleanse me from all unrighteousness. According to Romans 10:9, if I confess with my mouth the Lord Jesus, and believe in my heart that you raised Him from the dead, I shall be saved. I believe Jesus died for my sins, was buried, and was raised from the dead. Right now, I receive Him into my heart as my Lord and Savior. Please help me to grow in my knowledge of you and live for your glory. Amen.

It's that simple! Praise God! The heavens are rejoicing over **YOU**! (Luke 15:7)

# 21 Day Devotional & Study Guide

# INTRODUCTION

Thank you for purchasing the expanded version of **Clarity Is Divine** and investing in your emotional recovery. Hopefully, you have completed the book portion and are ready to commit to a process that will usher you into a true state of *Divine Clarity*. While navigating the twists and turns on this road called "Life", we encounter storms and detours that cause our sense of direction to become clouded and our reference points to become ambiguous. This can happen even when you surrender where you are going and how you are going to get there, to God. There is a divine peace that accompanies knowing exactly where you are—and *are not* for that matter. Imagine being lost and having someone to call for directions. You are confident that your contact knows the terrain that is unfamiliar to you and are anxious to get that person on the line. The first thing the person will ask is, "Where are you?" And if you are unable to answer the question, or cannot identify any landmarks or street signs, the person will not be able to help. Thank God the Father knows exactly where we are, even when we haven't a clue. Yet often times, to appreciate where you are going, you must be able to compare it to where you are. If you never knew you were bound, how can you appreciate being free? If you never knew you were lost, how can you appreciate being found? Many times, because we don't know how to process our pain, and feel overwhelmed by its antagonistic nature, we suppress it, and continue to trudge through life in a delusional state.

There is nothing wrong with admitting that you are not okay, that there are experiences that have damaged you and impact your moods, relationships and ability to trust God. There's safety in the truth. Those who worship God must worship Him in Spirit and in TRUTH (John 4:24). When you acknowledge where you are emotionally, you are able to be honest about your needs and where in your life, you need CLARITY.

It has been said that with focused attention, new habits can be formed in twenty-one days. Let's use the next twenty-one days for seeking God for truth, soul searching and discovery. Not for a moment do I want you to believe that you will achieve maximum emotional healing in just twenty-one days. That is NOT the purpose of this devotional. You can, however, decide which areas of your life, which disappointments, which painful areas you want to assign to twenty-one days of intense introspection and prayer. After spending the time in prayer, meditation and God's word, you will be well on your way to clearly understanding where you are in your search for divine guidance. You will be able to tell the One who knows every path that you can honestly identify the wrong turns and can appreciate the value in your *Divine Destination*.

Hopefully over time, you will revisit the devotional several times, assigning to and utilizing it for different areas of your life.

For each day, I have included *Clear Perspectives,* which are scriptures for you to read and meditate on before completing the *Clarifying Thoughts* section along with its writing assignment. Writing is a powerful exercise. Once you put a pen in your hand and release all fears and inhibitions, you may be surprised by what the heart has been pining to release and discover. I am excited about walking with you through these next twenty-one days. Don't expect it to be easy, but certainly expect it to be Godly! EXPECT GOD!!!

# WEEK ONE—DEAL WITH THE PAIN

Of course it is easier not to, but this is one of those many instances where the difficult thing to do is the best thing to do. Ignoring a problem doesn't make it go away.

Dealing with your pain strips it of its power to haunt you. Upon facing it, with God's help, you will confront and defeat the very burdens that have lurked over your shoulder for too long.

This experience is a lot like taking medicine. The taste can be bitter, but once you abandon fear and "get it over with" you will feel better and wish you had done it sooner. Let's Go!!!

# DAY ONE

**Forgive & Forget** . . .

Seems impossible right? Often times you will hear someone say, "I will forgive, but will never forget". What the person really means is that he or she will "say" they forgive, but will constantly rehearse and forcefully remember the offense in an effort to make sure the pain is never forgotten and remains directly associated with the person who caused it. That means the wound never heals and they relive the incident over and over to ensure that no one gets "off the hook" without punishment. There is a *fear* that if the pain isn't closely associated with the person's identity, one may become too comfortable or dismissive and thus positioned to be hurt, taken for granted or mistreated again.

Forgiveness simply means you are willing to abandon the belief that you are owed something. It means you are willing to no longer hold the offense against the person who hurt you. Let's say a friend hurts you. When you assess her character and consider the damage she is capable of doing based on her stance concerning a matter, her level of conviction (or lack thereof) or her level of maturity, you must determine how vulnerable you will be with her and what level of intimacy with her is "safe" for you. The aforementioned assessment is how you should protect yourself, instead of by staying angry or holding friend's fault against her. You aren't positioning yourself to be abused, because you forgave, you are positioning yourself to be free of the emotional and physical diseases that often result from bitterness and harboring hurt and unforgiveness. You are keeping your channel to God unclogged and leaving yourself available to love and be loved without the stench of your past contaminating your future.

Your past hurts have done ENOUGH damage and have held you captive for too long. We strip the past of its power today!!!

**Clear Perspectives**: Matthew 5:23-24 Matthew 5:44 Matthew 6:12 Matthew 6:14-15 Matthew 18:21&22 John 20:23 Hebrews 12:14&15

**Clarifying Thoughts:** After answering the questions, write down everything that has hurt you and rendered you fearful and doubtful. Attach the name(s) of the person(s) responsible and pray to God expressing your forgiveness for the individuals. If it is a difficult prayer, that is totally okay. Tell the Father that it is a difficult prayer for you, but because He requires forgiveness and His desires are more important to you than your justification for being angry, you are DECIDING to be obedient and forgive, no matter how uncomfortable it feels. It is a sacrifice He will honor.

In what ways has holding onto the offense hindered me?

What have I missed out on while my focus has been on the pain I was caused and the person who caused it?

Was there ANY part I was responsible for?

How long have I been hurting?

## DAY TWO

**No Tag-Alongs!**

Older siblings will definitely be able to relate to this analogy. Can you remember what it was like to wake up early, complete your chores with 100% effort, make sure you didn't leave any stone unturned and joyfully lay out an outfit—all in blissful preparation for plans you made weeks or months in advance to go out with friends, only to be told that you had to take your little brother or sister along with you? You did everything right! You finished your chores, cleaned with a fervency you NEVER waste on chores and waited to wear your special article of clothing at this special event. Now after being told you have to babysit or not go at all, you actually contemplate staying home, and you would if you didn't want to go out SO badly.

Although you adore your younger sibling, the issue with having the kid tag along is that you have to constantly consider his or her safety. Wherever you want to go, there has to be room for the "tag-along" too. Whatever you wish to participate in, the younger sibling would be attached to your hip, your mobility is hindered because the "tag-along" cannot run, jump, duck or climb as quickly as you (if that were to become necessary). Your plans are no longer about what you can handle, but what is appropriate, safe and realistic for your "tag-along".

There are some opportunities that faith and hope can access, but are not available for doubt, fear and bitterness. When the hurts from your past tag along, everyone notices, and only what or who is available to them (the doubt, fear and bitterness) are available to you. I believe most of us want what I like to call the Ephesians 3:20 blessings—the blessings that exceed the limits of our imaginations. The challenge is that those blessing are commensurate with the amount of power that is at work within us. The basic equation for power = strength / time, that is, strength over time. Have you been

121

consistently strong in your faith and in your belief in the word of God or have you been consistently inconsistent?

I want to do my work, my chores. I want to be in position to seize the opportunities that are available to all who BELIEVE God's promises, and I don't want to miss my appointment!!! How about you? When you love your younger sibling, you will allow him or her to tag along as often as necessary if it ensures their safety. But we have no allegiance to Satan's offspring that manifest in the form of negative thoughts and fears that hinder us, slow us down or disqualify us through a lack of faith. Those who believe God, believe God's promises, and in His ability to completely heal, know that we don't have to babysit these weights, hindrances and stumbling blocks. It's time to free our minds to think Godly thoughts and put aside everything that has resisted our forward movement. Decide today that you will not protect the tag-along(s) at your side. Your future is Greater than the hurt you have experienced.

**Clear Perspectives:** Hebrews 12:1 Philippians 4:8

**Clarifying Thoughts:** What thoughts seem to penetrate and sabotage your faith and peace when you begin to think about and anticipate the manifestation of God's promises?

What fears seem to accompany you on a consistent basis as it relates to making progress and experiencing the changes you believe God for?

# DAY THREE

## I am LOVABLE!!!

Even though life experiences may have sent the opposite message, the truth is that you are *"fearfully and wonderfully made"* and immensely ***LOVABLE***. When you've been forsaken, betrayed, abused and/or abandoned, this becomes very difficult to believe. Often times you have the thoughts, "If I'm so wonderful, why didn't my victimizer see it?" "Why wasn't I treated as if I am valuable?" "Why was I told that I am worthless?" "Why was I treated as if I didn't matter at all?"

It's quite liberating when we come to the realization that the way we were treated had NOTHING to do with our worth, but everything to do with the fact that some type of predator (whether sexual, emotional or physical) had access to us when we were not able to defend our safety. If you handed a one hundred dollar bill to someone who is foreign to our civilization or economic system, the person might assume that it is trash and throw it away, use it to put their chewed gum in, wipe their hands with it or toss it aside all together. BUT a person who knows better will see the value and understand that a tremendous blessing has been bestowed. It is all about perspective and what is familiar.

When someone doesn't recognize your value, it isn't because it doesn't exist, but rather because the person isn't equipped or socially sophisticated enough to recognize what or who stands before them. That has nothing to do with you. You might wonder how you have never been treated well throughout a series of relationships. At some point early on, you believed you weren't worth much. It may have been during your childhood. And as a result, you began to subconsciously communicate this to those with whom you have come into contact. Low self-esteem gives off a tantalizing scent to a predator on the prowl.

We must remember that the enemy of your faith uses those that he can as pawns. He knows your history and your weaknesses and he dispatches his reinforcements accordingly. Today is the day that you shut the door and deny him further access. Today you accept who God says that you are and decide to esteem His word and what He says about you higher than any past experience or any lies the enemy has ever whispered to you! Today you declare that you are not only valuable, but you are LOVABLE!! It's time to position yourself around those capable of recognizing that!

**Clear Perspectives:** Psalm 139

**Clarifying Thoughts:** When was the first time you remember feeling "unworthy" or "unlovable"?

What life event served as the catalyst that caused your sense of self-worth to spiral out of control?

List every person that has reinforced this false core belief?

# DAY FOUR

**This is NOT God's best for me!**

There's a wicked thought that accompanies abuse and it is launched from the depths of [the pit of] hell. When you're miserable and being treated badly, it is likened to being in a dreary house and looking out of the window at everyone else outside in the sun, moving about as if they haven't a care in the world. Through our lenses we look at those around us and compare our lives to theirs. We watch them laugh, smile and celebrate, and we wonder what landed us here. You ask, "Why is it that I am in this wretched and miserable situation while they are carefree and enjoying life? Why are they happily married while I endure abuse at home? Why do I try so much harder, but my only reward is pain?" At times it may seem that they were MADE for love and happiness while your existence is rooted in pain and suffering. When you hear the echoes of the voice of your distant faith that says "God is Good", the only conclusion you can draw from your predicament is that YOU must be bad. IT'S A LIE!!! Don't believe it!!! Consistent misery is not your lot in life. It isn't the life God created for you and it isn't the best He can do! There may not be a lot you can do to change the physical circumstances of your life TODAY, but you can certainly change your thoughts about it. Upon changing your thoughts you can change your perspective. Upon changing your perspective you can change your beliefs. Upon changing your beliefs, you can increase your faith and upon increasing your faith, you can change your expectations. You will find it to be amazing how much your actions reflect your expectations. Life CAN change! Things CAN be different. Once you believe God has better for you, you will be attentive to His directives and begin to move in the right direction! There is a BEST for you that has been waiting for you to BELIEVE!!!

**Clear Perspectives:** Psalm 139 AMP Jeremiah 29:11 John 10:10 Ephesians 2:8-10 AMP

**Clarifying Thoughts:** What aspects of my life am I dissatisfied with? Have I ever looked at someone else and assumed that their comfort or happiness was the result of them deserving it more than I do? What mental adjustments do I need to make to ensure that I begin to BELIEVE that the scriptures above apply to me too?

# DAY FIVE

**My Pain is a consequence, NOT my punishment.**

It isn't strange that you would think this way. We live by a seed/harvest system. While growing up, we are trained to believe that there are rewards for good behaviors and punishments for bad. Naturally when we feel badly or when something negative happens to us, we associate it with a punishment. Consider the fact that based on the *Law of the Harvest* (seed/harvest system), God doesn't always have to intervene. There are consequences to our negative actions. And in context, negative actions are actions that aren't representative of His way of doing things. Negative actions reap negative consequences. Understanding this will help you to understand that the God who loves you so much and wants you to get it right, was desiring for you to do the right thing so that you wouldn't have to endure the consequences of a bad decision. When we hurt, He hurts with us. He would much rather we be blessed. We must realize that when we CHOOSE wrong, we agree to the consequences they produce. It's that simple.

Consider the following scenario: You tell your five year old to use a plastic cup instead of a glass because you know he is prone to dropping things. In his disobedience, he uses a glass, breaks it and cuts his hands. He sees the blood and runs to you crying. Would you be happy about your son's misfortune? I think not! As a parent, even though he was disobedient, you aren't happy about the consequence. You would certainly clean the wounds and comfort him, but the consequences he endured are a bi-product of his actions.

Maybe you engaged in an unhealthy relationship because you wanted to be loved. Maybe you didn't want to fornicate, but you knew it was the only way the person would remain in a relationship with you. Maybe you continued a relationship that God told you to end, because you loved the person. While wanting love isn't a bad thing in and of itself, it becomes a problem when the desire becomes more important than pleasing God. When protecting our relationship with a significant other takes priority over us protecting our relationship with God through obedience, that person has become our *god*. That person has become more important to us than God! Does that vex Him? Yes! Does He know the decision will harm you? Yes. We all have free will and as He watches you pick up the glass that will break and cut you, He simply waits for you to cry and run to Him. He doesn't turn His back on you. He welcomes you and cleans you up. He's not punishing you, He's just waiting for you to see the error in your ways. At this time, you can repent (apologize and turn from your erroneous ways) and begin again! The consequences may not disappear, but He will help and strengthen you through them. One day, the five year old matures and realizes the parent knew best and wasn't trying to keep him from enjoying his beverage, but rather the parent simply wanted it to be a SAFE and enjoyable experience. He loves you more than any parent loves her five year old. There is protection in doing things His way and blessings too!!

**Clear Perspectives:** Luke 11:11&12 Hebrews 4:15

**Clarifying Thoughts:** Where have I willfully participated in a situation that wasn't pleasing to God that ended up causing me great pain? Did I know better? Upon taking responsibility for MY part, how can I do things differently next time?

# DAY SIX

**The Law of Attraction**—You don't attract the same experience or person because you deserve it, but because it seeks familiarity.

One of my absolute favorite scriptures is John 14:30. The Amplified Version reads: I will not talk with you much more, for the prince (evil genius, ruler) of the world is coming. And he has no claim on Me. [He has nothing in common with Me; there is nothing in Me that belongs to him, and he has no power over Me.]

Expect to attract whatever is inside of you. Isn't it interesting how often one continues to attract the same "type" of suitor? It can be a different circumstance, a different year, a different location, but a person with the same set of issues. How many times have you found that your father was a womanizer, and now you attract men with the same issue? How many people grow up in homes with a parent who suffers from alcoholism and ends up marrying someone with the same disease that almost ripped their family apart? It isn't because you went seeking after an individual that would give you the same woes. You simply attracted a person that has a "home" in you. It's a situation where "your chaos matches my chaos, so let's come together and live chaotically". This happens unintentionally. Don't you find that it's the people you have something in common with that make you feel the most comfortable—the most "at home"?

That said, put that finger down that has been pointing at everyone "else" as you blame "them" for the pain you feel. Today, we forgive our caretakers for modeling dysfunctional behavior in front of us when we were impressionable children. Today, we take responsibility for not having healed before becoming romantically involved with anyone. Today, we choose to get cleaned up on the inside, so that it is the peace, love and security on the inside of us that attracts the same from someone else.

Anything on the inside of you that has its roots in the enemy (strife, jealousy, lust, etc.), he has legal access to. Strife belongs to him. Jealousy belongs to him. Lust belongs to him. And if he

129

wants to access it, or use it, he has every right. Basically, in the aforementioned verse, Jesus is saying, "he has no rights to me". When nothing in you belongs to him, he has to keep walking. He gets NO ACCESS. That is something to think about. Doesn't it make you want to get all cleaned up so that he has to keep walking past you, because he has no door to walk through; no personal property to put his grimy hands on?

Today our prayer is that there is nothing in us that would corroborate with the enemy. We want to be on the Lord's side COMPLETELY!

**Clear Perspectives:** 2 Corinthians 4:7-10 Galatians 5:19-21

**Clarifying Thoughts:** What areas in my thought life and social life do I still need to yield to God? What undesirable traits in others do I continue to attract? What personal experiences can I attribute them to?

## DAY SEVEN

Rest & Vent. You don't have to work today. Just write what you feel. Experience the freedom of expressing yourself.

# WEEK 2—HOW DID I GET HERE?

Have you ever reached a destination or completed a task, but couldn't remember the drive or the steps you took to complete the task? So many times, there has been so much on my mind when I had completed something or arrived somewhere, but couldn't quite remember the process. We can get so accustomed to doing certain things that the steps it takes to get them accomplished are second nature to us.

When it comes to behavior patterns, most of us just know "it's the way we are", but haven't given much thought to why—or what experience(s) shaped our choice of methods we use to deal with life. It's time to take a look at the foundation. You will see where there are cracks and objects that obstruct its integrity. There is work involved, but a structure with a sound foundation is one that can stand the test of time!

# DAY EIGHT

**Grieve . . .**

*It won't come out if it never comes up.*

What is that thing you suppress EVERYDAY? You've gotten so used to hiding it, you forget that it's hidden.

Most of us have become masters of disguise. It has to be a really bad day, I mean a REALLY bad day for the outside world to be able to tell from our appearance that we are suffering. We still put on make-up, get things done and juggle our many roles and responsibilities. Many of us have become too good at "pain management". Those who abuse alcohol, drugs and gambling aren't the only ones with addictive behaviors. What about when one eats, not because of hunger, but because it makes one feel better? How about the trip to the mall for a little "retail therapy"? Nowadays you don't even have to get up from your seat (or bed) since many of us even shop online. And you, the exercise bandit, you aren't getting away! There are many different addictions and different manifestations of the same issue.

Hurt doesn't feel good. Hurt hurts. And most of us will avoid it at all costs—especially when there is nothing we can do about it. The problem with our addictions is that we are running to a "source" to numb our pain instead of the Source who can cure our pain! We must learn to trust God enough to say "This hurts. It makes me feel rejected, lonely, ugly and hopeless and I don't want to feel this way anymore." I have to ask you today if you honestly believe that He is enough God to heal your pain? When you give yourself permission to grieve and toss to Him every hurt and concern, you are releasing the burden of carrying them. When you allow the hurts to bubble up and out, you look up and realize you haven't gained weight, broken the support beams in your closet or put yourself in financial debt. You gave the pain to the One who was able to do something about it. It's what our Father calls a "Fair Exchange". I so love Him for that!

**Clear Perspectives:** Hebrews 4:15 1 Peter 5:7

**Clarifying Thoughts:** Ask God today to reveal to you every hurt that you haven't released to Him. Every pain that you have covered with sweets, food, clothing, cosmetics, gambling, alcohol, cigarettes, drugs or anything else that you used in place of His loving arms. Ask forgiveness for not letting Him be your burden bearer. Write down every pain and consciously cast it to Him. And whatever you do, don't take it back! Do this as many times as it takes.

# DAY NINE

*The first time in this relationship I felt the pain and the first time (in life) I remember feeling the pain.*

Often times our "triggers" have the effect that they do and are able to motivate us to react, because they are reminiscent of a previous experience; typically, a previous *painful* experience. When we find that we are triggered, yet only deal with the situation at hand, it is like re-injuring an old wound and placing another band-aid on it without irrigating and cleaning it so that it can continue to heal properly. Have you ever noticed that occasionally the pain that you feel is much more intense than the situation that triggered you? Old wounds that never healed properly continue to be problematic. When a bone is broken, it has to be set properly so that it can heal properly. If not, over time you can continue to experience pain, a limp, limited mobility, etc.

**Clear Perspectives:** Psalm 27:13 2 Corinthians 4:6-18

**Clarifying Thoughts:** Today, prayerfully consider your mobility and seek where it is limited. Where does your "flow" become disrupted? What causes you to come to a screeching halt? What triggers can occur that cause you to go back to the familiar place of pain, insecurity, abandonment and shame? When you identify the place(s), go deeper. Search out the onset of those feelings. In finding the FIRST time, we can overwrite the memory with the love of God. With enough practice, what used to trigger pain, will trigger a tremendous sense of promise. May we come to a place where when we have to look back, it doesn't make us bitter, but better! God is making you BETTER!!! Clean wounds heal with no infection!

## DAY TEN

***When I felt it as a child what message was sent that I believed?***

Memories send messages. How many times have we blamed our battle with fear or low self-esteem on our previous marriage or a previous relationship? We rehearse and recite how badly someone hurt us, despite the fact that we loved that person so much. We tell the story over and over again about how we gave the person everything, but he or she left us only a fraction of the person we were before the relationship. We relive the pain and humiliation of the "relationship gone bad" and perceive ourselves as victims of unfavorable circumstance.

The truth is that our emotional challenges didn't begin with the failed relationship. It was pre-existing emotional hang-ups that positioned us in relationships that were not going to be healthy for us. If I don't believe I deserve to be treated well, I position myself and remain in relationships where I am not treated well. Even worse, in relationship, we send messages that we will accept such behavior. In essence, we have said (indirectly of course), "Although it is obvious you are not honest with me, I will proceed in building a relationship with you, because quite frankly, I don't feel I deserve honesty." Or "I don't really feel I have value or that my body is God's temple, therefore, I will allow you to misuse it and abuse it, because quite frankly, I feel YOU are a prize and I don't want to be left alone with my horrible self."

Our adult relationships didn't teach us to think this way, but have served as a platform for us to act out what we really believe [about ourselves]. This is a critical revelation. Changing our thoughts about ourselves and what we deserve will change our beliefs. Changing our beliefs will change our behaviors. Changing our behaviors will change our patterns. Changing our patterns will change our susceptibility. Changing our susceptibility will change our relationships! Are you ready for a chain reaction?

**Clear Perspectives:** Psalms 139 AMP

**Clarifying Thoughts:** Yesterday our focus was identifying the genesis of our feelings of pain, insecurity, rejection, abandonment, fear and whatever additional dispositions have emotionally [and possibly physically] crippled us. These initial experiences caused us to believe something about ourselves that isn't in line with God's word nor what He has spoken about us. Today, write down the belief that originated as a bi-product of the emotional trauma you experienced. Ask God to help you identify what you began to believe and then write how it is in contrast to the word of God. Cross out the old belief and rehearse the new one! You are no longer the victim of the victim that harmed you. You are fearfully and wonderfully made and armed with the strength and value of God's truth!

# DAY ELEVEN

*During the years after the genesis—how did I "act out" my private belief system?*

Isn't it exciting to have identified exactly where we have strayed from the truth of God's word? The fact that you have begun to identify the lies the enemy fed to you and have come to recognize how you corroborated with the enemy in weaving them into your emotional framework is life-altering. Every erroneous belief God has helped you identify, He will help you replace. Be patient with yourself as this is a process. Over the years, you have formed habits that are rooted in your false core belief system (Chapter 4).

Now that the false core beliefs have been identified, it is time for you to walk in faith and be intentional about obeying the word of God [concerning yourself) in thought, word and deed! Would you cast your pearl necklace to a pig? Absolutely not! You handle it with care and protect it from being damaged because of the value you place on it. I don't want to make it seem this should be an easy task. Think about how many decades your marred self-image has sat in the driver's seat. False core beliefs are like concrete that is poured over TIME. It hardens again and again over time; being reinforced by layered betrayals and occurrences. This isn't an exercise that you will master the first time. Like any other habit it must be reinforced through repetition. Rejoice in the fact you now know what has kept you feeling so defeated. Praise God that you are grateful that the TIME has come for this change! It is TIME to protect your mind, body, emotions and spirit the same way you would that pearl necklace. Say this aloud: *I am valuable, therefore, I present myself in a respectable way. I carry the virtue and light of Christ, therefore, I will concentrate on alliances and behaviors that reflect the respect that I have for myself and the investment God has made in me. He says I'm worth it!!! Who am I to argue?*

**Clear Perspectives:** Psalms 138:8 Psalms 139:23-24 Matthew 7:6

**Clarifying Thoughts:** Today ask God to reveal every way you have acted out your false core beliefs. Write them down and then write down behaviors and habits that reflect your belief in everything God has spoken over you.

As often as you need to, revisit what you have written. When you are being mistreated or when you feel triggered, remember that you may not be able to control the circumstance or the actions of another, but you CAN control how you react moving forward! What a wonderful life! Amen

# DAY TWELVE

*The last time I felt the "ache" in the most recent relationship-how deep was the hurt?*

There are some relationships that you can't very well walk away from. For instance, there may be someone in your family that is so engulfed with pain and so unyielding to God's grace, that the person can't stop being hurtful. No matter how unpleasant it feels, we have to continue to love the unlovable, interact with the less favorable and attend functions that leave you wishing you were scrubbing a toilet somewhere instead. On this path to clarity, it shouldn't be your endeavor to change others, but to change the intensity with which others can affect you. Just because you feel better about yourself doesn't mean that others will change their behavior. The key here is making sure that you no longer internalize their behavior and feel badly about yourself as a result of their behavioral shortcomings.

One person in particular used to manipulate me by calling me "selfish". Anytime I didn't do what he wanted me to do [for him], he would accuse me of being selfish. He knew that I didn't want to be labeled as such and that his opinion of me mattered. So, he would ask me to do something that required me to overextend myself; I would decline, he would accuse me of being selfish and then I would buckle. But once I became clear about who I am, who I am not and that I am only required to do what God requires of me, I stopped dancing to the beat of his drum. At first, standing my ground was painful, because I had to endure the insult. But as I believed it less and less, it just rolled off of my back. Eventually it mattered to me as much as someone telling me I was wearing blue, when in fact I was wearing yellow. The key here is beginning to believe what God says about you more than what you told yourself or what others have said about you.

The change in my reaction didn't happen overnight, but after each incident, I would notice how it affected me less and less.

Eventually, he stopped saying it all together, as the tactic didn't work anymore. SCORE!

**Clear Perspectives:** Jeremiah 29:11-13 Jeremiah 33:3 Luke 9:5 1 Peter 3:16

**Clarifying Thoughts:** What am I having a hard time believing about myself? When I read the scriptures and what God has said about me, what false core beliefs are being threatened? Who is it in my life that reinforces my false core beliefs? What changes do I need to make so that their comments and actions will no longer adversely affect me?

# DAY THIRTEEN

*False Humility—Though the person shouldn't take advantage of your weakness, you left the door open. The robber shouldn't rob, BUT if you don't lock him out, don't be surprised if he comes in.*

Let me explain. It's much easier to identify with the role of a victim than it is to take responsibility for actions and dispositions that have caused us to hurt ourselves and others. Have you ever repeatedly put yourself in harm's way in the name of forgiveness, when forgiveness doesn't actually require you to be careless with yourself? Have you ever made the statement that you were simply kind to someone and they continuously took advantage of your kindness? This is false humility. It causes you to give yourself a badge for good behavior, when in fact the behavior was unwise and a tool you used to justify remaining in a hurtful place, blame someone else for the pain you felt as a result, and to avoid taking responsibility for any of it. Humility allows us to submit to the word of God, including what He says about us. If the word of God states, such as in Psalm 139:14 that you are "fearfully and wonderfully made", yet when you argue that you are terribly flawed and useless, you are usurping the word of God. Your ***pride*** is exalting what YOU think above the truth God has spoken. You thought it sounded humble, when in fact it is insulting to our Creator. Operating in truth means that we must operate in tandem with the word of God. On this path to clarity, you will need to take responsibility for yourself. As a helpless child, you didn't have much say over the situations that would affect you for years to come. Now you do! It is much easier to sit back and enjoy a pity party, but if you are going to agree with God, you must believe Him and then it must be followed up by actions.

**Clear Perspectives:** Psalms 139:14 Matthew 7:5 2 Corinthians 10:5 James 2:17

**Clarifying Thoughts:** Where have I shunned responsibility by operating in false humility? In what ways was my behavior contrary to the word of God?

# DAY FOURTEEN

Rest & Vent. You don't have to work today. Just write what you feel. Experience the freedom of expressing yourself.

# WEEK THREE—GET UP!

One of my favorite accounts in the Bible is the one of the Prodigal Son (Luke 15:11-32). After the son made his mistakes and suffered as a result, verse seventeen reads "he came to himself". After wallowing in self-pity and regret, he remembered who he was in relation to his father. And once he remembered, he got up!

You have experienced the hurt and more recently you have come to terms with it. Now it's time to "Get Up", go to the Father and confidently allow the rest of your story to be written. It doesn't end here. There's MORE!

# DAY FIFTEEN

**BREATHE . . . .**

Before we start today, I would like you to give yourself a hug. Go ahead! Put the book down and hug yourself! Say aloud: *I am worth all of the work that I am doing.* Now, I want you to make SURE you believe it. Facing the truth isn't easy. If you completed the devotional assignments last week, that is a GREAT indication that you are ready to do your part in whatever is necessary to have the life full of peace and joy that at one point seemed to be in the far distance. Any time we draw closer to truth, we draw closer to God. And any time we draw closer to God, we draw closer to His attributes. How can one come into contact with the master Creator and not be changed? Last week, the line was drawn, the separation was made. You made a clear distinction between what was God and what was self. You reflected upon your past choices and you wrote down the behavior patterns that were in opposition to God's nature. You did all of this in an effort to position yourself to CHOOSE GOD each time you are presented with a temptation to draw back, repeat old patterns or listen to your voice that speaks over His at times. Good work! And a LOT of work it was! Today is all about really sticking your stilettos/heels into this [new] ground. No matter what/who comes and goes you must be resolved to believe God about everything He says about your life, your value and who He created you to be. When you aren't treated well, you can be tempted to feel a sense of low self-worth. If a so-called friend goes AWOL, those old feelings of abandonment may resurface. Doing the emotional work doesn't in any way guarantee that there will never be invitations to the past. But a *self* rooted in truth, and stronger in Christ will not accept the invitation. Stand your ground.

**Clear Perspectives:** Romans 7:8 Hebrews 10:38

**Clarifying Thoughts:** When you are walking in complete freedom from the sting of the emotional turbulence of your past, what type of life do you see for yourself? Think BIG.

# DAY SIXTEEN

### Unfamiliar Necessities . . .

Forgiveness takes love. On Day One you were faced with the challenge of forgiving others and it wasn't something you were capable of doing in your own strength. When you have been harmed, it is difficult to release the charge against the assailant, even when the perpetrator is yourself. After accepting responsibility for my choices and realizing that my behavior patterns were the reason things were still the way they were in my life and relationships, I became so angry with myself. Repeatedly I scolded myself for not having done better. I rehearsed how much TIME I lost in unfruitful cycles.

In prayer one day, the Holy Spirit whispered to me not to be tricked out of ungratefulness. If you've been in bondage for ten consecutive years and are liberated on the first day of the eleventh year, thank God for freedom. Thank God the bondage didn't last another day, another week, another month or year. Thank God there was a limit! We can become so focused on the past that we forget to praise Him and remain in a thankful state AFTER the handcuffs have fallen off. No matter what you suffered, or how long, be grateful that the season, the trial, the situation (whatever it was) had an expiration date! Be grateful for the fact that you have a chance at something new and refreshing. Sadly, some people died in their bondage, but you didn't!

Have you ever noticed how when animals that have been in captivity for a prolonged period of time have their cages opened, they don't leave the cage? They became so accustomed to being in captivity that they don't know how to walk freely. Their desire for the "outside" died somewhere along the way. Being bound is bad enough. Don't be FREE and bound! Walk in your freedom. Position yourself to be blessed through praise and expectancy.

It may SEEM late, but no matter what phase of life you find yourself, it isn't too late for God to "do exceeding abundantly above all that you can ask or think". Here's the catch: what He does will be according to His power that works in you. Don't allow bitterness, resentment, misery and disappointment to prohibit His power from working within you. They are in direct opposition to the love of God. It is a challenge to cast them aside when they have been steady companions. But they serve as anchors for unforgiveness and aren't welcomed on this journey. They overstayed their welcome! You're on a path of clarity, joy and fulfillment.

On this journey you need new companions, love and trust. Love will empower you to forgive yourself and trust will empower you to remain confident that He will finish well, the wonderful life transformation that has started.

**Clear Perspectives:** Philippians 1:6 Philippians 2:13

**Clarifying Thoughts:** In what areas do I need to forgive myself? In what areas does it seem that I am getting a "late start" due to the time I served in an emotional prison? Write the answers to these questions and then write the new beliefs concerning your future that you will adopt through faith. As many times that you feel your gratitude slipping away, you are free to revisit your vision. Thank God for journals!

# DAY SEVENTEEN

Have you ever dieted? If you were successful, it was because you were consistent. One day of restricting yourself from eating the foods you desire can feel like the longest twenty-four hours imaginable. After a few days you begin to study yourself in the mirror, looking for signs of change. The reality is, it takes longer than a few days. Many people who have lost weight dieting will tell you that when they stopped focusing on the change and focused on successfully managing their regimen, change followed. Looking for it didn't cause it to happen any sooner. Consistently following the diet, resulted in the change they wanted to see.

As uncomfortable as it may have been to abstain from candy and potato chips, once you zipped the pair of jeans you couldn't fit before, would you agree it was worth the trouble? The process was difficult, but worth the effort. The results were worth the process.

We spend so much time praying that a person we are in a relationship with will change. If only this person did that and that person did this, things would run so much more smoothly. Looking and waiting for others to change is a lot like constantly looking in the mirror while you're on a diet. It can seem like all of your waiting is to no avail. You will find that if you focus on the steps you have committed to in this devotional, one day you will look up and realize that you feel completely different about your relationships. Even if it is because you are the one who changed!

I have found that I have enough to work on to keep myself busy. Often you will find that after focusing on your part and what God is requiring of you, your perspective changes completely. Sometimes God doesn't change the situation before He changes us. He allows us to mature through circumstances so that we can successfully navigate through life's next obstacle.

As you walk the path of clarity you will form new, healthier relationships. You will also have to maintain some of your previous relationships. But because so much has changed in you, because there is more peace, more joy and more resolve, you won't be affected the same way by actions that would have previously sent you into a tailspin. As your boundaries become clear, you will know when to give and when to take, when to move forward and when to retreat, when you are safe and when you are not. There is a space where you dwell alone with your Creator, Protector and Counselor. While His love will flow in and out of you as you embrace others, care for and nurture relationships with others, He alone will sit on the throne of your heart. In THIS relationship is complete safety and security.

**Clear Perspectives:** Psalms 40:2-4 Psalms 91

**Clarifying Thoughts:** Today take inventory of your relationships. Ask God to help you identify the relationships that are supported by the framework of your false core beliefs. This isn't for the purpose of throwing anyone away, but so that you will be clear about how to pray about each alliance. Ask God to reveal to you what potholes to avoid and how He can ultimately get the glory out of the relationship(s). Write about what is revealed to you.

# DAY EIGHTEEN

**Limited Capacities . . .**

Last year my nephew completed Kindergarten. For him, advancing to the first grade was a REALLY big deal. I noticed that after the school year began, he referred to the kindergarteners at his school as babies. His mother explained to him that they were only one year younger than him. His response was, "they're loud and don't even know to stop playing when the teacher calls them." Didn't he just learn these things last year?

Sometimes because we know better, we expect others to do better. Chapter Ten opened with "Without Jesus, everyone is dysfunctional!" We cannot forget that some of the worst offenders in our lives have been people who never learned any better. There are some people who "love(d)" us in the most dysfunctional manner, but a manner that reflects all they've known nonetheless. There are some that clearly don't have the capacity [yet] to do better simply because they're perspective hasn't been broadened. This is where you have to be careful not to be too critical. Does this mean that you have no choice but to suffer recurring disappointments? Not necessarily. While exercising patience, you can protect yourself by appropriating your expectations. Don't expect more from someone than you know they have the capacity to give. Some behaviors persist until there is an emotional evolution. If you remain realistic about the platform of understanding from which a person operates, many of their habits and behaviors won't surprise you; thus you will experience less disappointment. You may desire better for them, but in loving them selflessly, your desire for them to grow will be out of concern and a yearning to see them at their best, as opposed to being because it is beneficial for you in the relationship.

**Clear Perspectives:** Proverbs 3:5 Matthew 7:1-5

**Clarifying Thoughts:** Ask God in prayer to help you identify where in your relationships, you have continuously set yourself up to be disappointed. Where have you not paid attention to a person's capacity to execute sound judgment? In what ways can you redirect your expectations?

# DAY NINETEEN

*Are you willing to go alone?*

Often times, during our moments of spiritual revelation and emotional bliss, we make all kinds of powerful confessions: "All I need is you Lord! "Send me and I will go!" "I want whatever you want for me!" "Show me what you want from me, and whatever it is, I will do it!" Do any of these expressions sound familiar? They are SO faithful in nature and seem like everything a "good Christian" would say. The challenge is that many of us express these sentiments during moments of intense praise and emotional determination without having first considered if we're willing to pay the price required to follow through with any of it.

When we start out on our Christian journey, we do so anticipating that all will be well in the world. We don't consider that our relationships may become strained or that the support systems on which we previously depended will begin to buckle. I didn't know when I accepted Christ that certain friends and family members wouldn't like the change they saw in me. I didn't expect that some would begin to persecute me for hanging my life on a belief that [with their finite mind], they were incapable of recognizing as truth.

Committing my life to the gospel of Jesus Christ required more than I initially bargained for. This is one of the reasons that CLARITY is so important. If you aren't clear about why you love Christ and how you would be absolutely lost without Him, choosing to honor your relationship with Him above any other relationship will be taxing, painful and difficult. Without clarity, you can easily grant someone else His seat. The disciple of Christ has to be willing to forsake all others, even yourself for the agenda and will of God to be done. You have to be willing to "go" if no one follows you, accompanies you or agrees with you.

When you CLEARLY understand that your relationship with Him is personal and sustainable without involvement from anyone else, you will understand the danger of there being too much involvement from anyone else. No human being is capable of having the integrity, faithfulness, love, grace or mercy it takes to share the throne of your heart with the living God. Becoming divinely clear has never been about primarily securing, fixing or strengthening a relationship with anyone else. It has always been about filtering and assigning to its proper place any and everything that has encumbered your allegiance to the One who gives you life and hope. You may have to go alone, but with Him, you're in the BEST company.

**Clear Perspectives:** 1 Corinthians 1:18 1 Corinthians 2:14 Romans 1:16

**Clarifying Thoughts:** Today, ask God to reveal to you which relationships tend to steer you away from His voice and His will that He communicates to you. Ask Him to show you who competes with Him for the #1 place in your heart. Write freely and honestly. Lastly write the fears that are associated with releasing your emotional dependence on others and allowing Him to be your FIRST love in thought, word and deed.

# DAY TWENTY

**It's a Process.**

Be patient with yourself. Love on yourself and keep reminding yourself that you can master these steps and will be better for having completed these reading and writing assignments. The purpose of this twenty-one day devotional isn't to have you look in the mirror on the twenty-first day and not recognize yourself, but to assist you in shifting your paradigm. Your paradigm is your platform or process by which you filter information, make decisions, and arrive at conclusions.

The mind undergoing a transformative process is absolutely essential for Christian growth. So, remember that any transformation happens in stages. Hopefully you will revisit this guide and repeat the steps as often as necessary until you notice that your thoughts, beliefs, behaviors, patterns, relationships and life overall have shifted. This isn't a sprint, but a marathon. Have you ever cooked something too quickly at a high temperature and noticed that while it looked done on the outside, the inside hadn't cooked thoroughly? We are capable of *appearing* mature, emotionally stable, and CLEAR, while being incapable of actually producing the spiritual fruit that reflects such maturity [and discipline].

You don't want to be the person that uses the correct verbiage, but doesn't have the fortitude and resolve to stand for what is confessed.

The emotional framework wasn't built overnight. It will take courage, tenacity and consistency to demolish it and the same to replace it with an infrastructure that glorifies God and positions you for spiritual and emotional fulfillment. The fact that you have persisted and remained committed to these twenty-one days indicates that you are not only equipped, but ready to receive the mysteries and treasures that accompany the abundant life Christ died for you to live.

Being *CLEAR* has tremendous benefits. You will have confidence in your authority through God to command life, instead of life circumstances commanding you! Unfavorable circumstances have occurred in everyone's life. And though God didn't create them or need them to get the glory, He is sovereign enough to cause and require them to work for your good! There is a lesson to take from every trauma, a victory to seize from every failure and a testimony from both, that you can use to encourage someone else.

I always encourage others not to struggle free of charge. Require a blessing to come forth from your trials!!!

Think about it, confusion caused you to recognize your need for *divine clarity* and *divine clarity* is going to completely transform your life!

**Clear Perspectives:** John 10:10 Romans 8:28

2 Corinthians 1:4 2 Timothy 3:1-5 1 Peter 2:9

**Clarifying Thoughts:** Today, breathe quietly for a few moments with absolutely no interruptions. Quiet your thoughts. Think of a few people or things that make you smile, memories included. Say this aloud: *God is good and I can trust Him.* Now write down various concerns that have surfaced throughout these twenty-one days. Make sure to include the things that seem too much for you to handle. For your last line, write: *I give all of this to God. May He direct me however He pleases, and I will surrender.* We have to trust His methods. What we were doing beforehand, *CLEARLY* wasn't working!

# DAY TWENTY-ONE

## "HALLELUJAH ANYHOW!!!"

I can laugh about it now, but when I was a new convert that expression really annoyed me. I couldn't understand why people believed it made any sense at all to praise God when something went wrong. Yet, of course as we mature, we begin to look for Him in any situation. Even when we cannot identify His involvement, we know two things: it likely could have been worse, and He will be with us through whatever circumstances arise.

Life circumstances can be difficult and dirty . . . no surprise there. The good news is that no matter what happens during our **temporary** stay on Earth, when we belong to Christ, an eternity of pure love, joy and healing are ours—FOREVER! When we look at the big picture, WE WIN!!! So, we can "HALLELUJAH ANYHOW!!!"

Moving forward, may you always make a conscientious effort to abide in His love. God's love is absolutely perfect. It is never strained or fragmented. It's just PERFECT. Scripture tells us "perfect love casts out fear." This means that His perfect love banishes the fear of failure, pain, loneliness, loss, mistakes, people, even the unknown.

We are also promised in His word that nothing or no one can separate us from His love. I don't know about you, but for me, that is INCREDIBLY comforting. There's the promise that He won't reject me or one day be "over me". He loves me with an everlasting love! Who doesn't want to experience being loved like that?

When I consider all that we have going for us and all that is ours from now through eternity, I understand better and better why the Apostle Paul wrote that "the sufferings of this present time are not worth being compared to the glory that will be revealed to us, in us and for us." (paraphrased)No matter what, WE WIN!!!

For those of you who desire such, today marks a new beginning. You have an opportunity to do things differently with a completely different outlook. I am SO very proud of you! Not just for completing the twenty-one day devotional, but because you survived and loved yourself and others enough to take actions steps toward being stronger, better and wiser. Anytime you commit to positive change, you are committing to be stronger, better and wiser! You are a masterpiece!

**Clear Perspectives:** Romans 8:18 2 Corinthians 4:17

**Clarifying Thoughts:** Today, breathe quietly for a few moments with absolutely no interruptions. Quiet your thoughts. Back already? Keep going a little longer . . . Now, after reading the *Clear Perspectives,* write freely. How do you feel? You may even want to glance back at what you wrote on Day One. I believe you will notice a different tone. And guess what?! If you keep loving yourself and if you stay committed to the transformative power of God's word for your life, it will only get better from here! God is good and *Clarity Is Divine.* Blessings, Peace & Love!

~Kelsi

# About the Author

KELSI MARIE ARCENEAUX is a native of Berkeley, CA. She is currently an evangelist and radio broadcaster based in the San Francisco Bay Area. After publishing *Clarity Is Divine* as an article in 2012, and in response to the reactions it produced, ministry associates and friends encouraged her to expound, to give readers access to her process of restoration. She has a passion for seeing people emotionally healed and freed from spiritual and emotional bondage.

After reading *Clarity is Divine*, feel free to share your feedback and testimonies. She would love to hear from you!

Twitter: @kelsimarie510

Facebook: Clarity Is Divine

Website: http://www.kelsimarie.com

For feedback or speaking engagements, contact Kelsi Marie at: info@kelsimarie.com